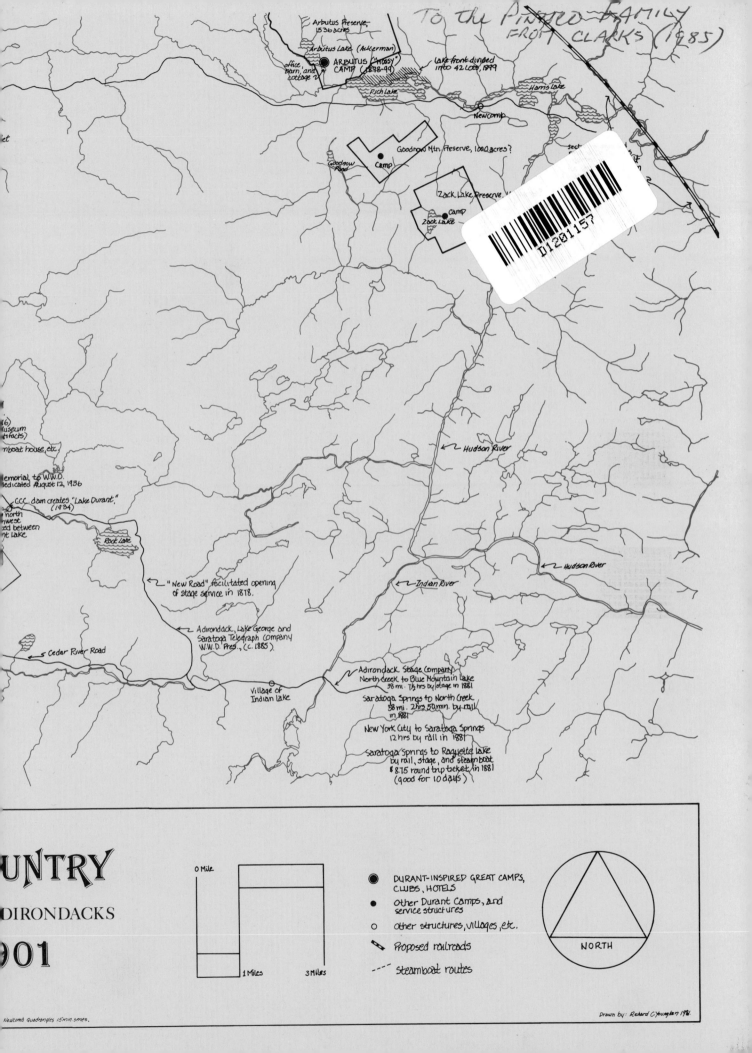

DURANT

DURANT

The Fortunes and Woodland Camps of a Family in the Adirondacks

CRAIG GILBORN

NORTH COUNTRY BOOKS • Sylvan Beach, N.Y.

In Cooperation with
THE ADIRONDACK MUSEUM • Blue Mountain Lake, N.Y.

To the memory of
Harold K. Hochschild
(1892 — 1981)

© Copyright 1981
by
The Adirondack Museum
Blue Mountain Lake, N.Y.

Library of Congress Catalog Card Number 81-81438

ISBN 0-932052-24-X

Manufactured in the United States of America
by Canterbury Press, Rome, New York

Acknowledgments

This book tells of a prominent New York family and of the "grand camps" which were built by members of the family in the Adirondack wilds of northern New York State during the last quarter of the nineteenth century. Segments of the story about the Durant family, its conflicts and ambitious plans for establishing a resort empire, appeared in most issues of the weekly newspaper *The Hamilton County News* between July, 1979 and February, 1980. To HCN's capable and genial editor, Mr. George List, the author offers his thanks for an opportunity to restore to the people of Hamilton County an historical chapter in which their parents and grandparents were the participants. To the family narrative has been added descriptions of the village-like camps which borrowed from the log and bark-covered shanties of the guide, trapper and lumberjack, and evolved, under the direction of William West Durant, into the prototype of the Camp Beautiful.

The author expresses appreciation also to the following for information, guidance and illustrations: Mr. James R. Bird, Miss Clara O. A. Bryere, Mr. and Mrs. John C. Collins, Mr. and Mrs. Patrick F. Collins, Mr. and Mrs. Edward Comstock, Jr., Mr. Bruce N. Coulter, Mrs. Butler Collins Cunningham, Mr. William Distin, Jr., Ms. Mary Ellen Domblewski, Mrs. Kenneth Durant, Mr. Frederick Clark Durant, III, Mr. George Fuge, Mr. James Fynmore, Dr. Anthony N. B. Garvan, Mrs. Francis P. Garvan, Dr. John C. A. Gerster, Dr. John W. Gerster, Drs. Howard and Barbara Glaser-Kirschenbaum, Mrs. Francis Havinga, Mr. and Mrs. Robert Igoe, Mr. Harry A. Inman, Dr. Harvey Kaiser, Mr. John S. Kathan, Mr. Richard Linke, Mr. John Mahaffy, Mr. Paul Malo, Ms. Carolyn A. Davis of the George Arents Research Library for Special Collections at Syracuse University, Mr. William C. Tierson, Mr. Norman J. Van Valkenburgh, Mr. Arthur Wareham, Mr. Sidney S. Whelan, Jr., Mr. and Mrs. C. V. Whitney and Mr. Richard Youngken.

Papers, photographs and artifacts have come to the Adirondack Museum over the years through the generosity of the Durant family. All are now deceased, and some might not agree with the interpretation in these pages, but all, including the principal figure, William West Durant, should be acknowledged: Mr. Frederick Clark Durant, Jr., Mr. Harrison Durant, Mr. Kenneth Durant, Mrs. William West (Annie Cotton) Durant, and Mrs. Bromley Durant Seeley. There were a number of Durant documents among the papers given to the Museum's library by a Herkimer attorney, Charles E. Synder, in 1965.

The staff of the Adirondack Museum have been faithful sources of assistance, notably Ms. Tracy Meehan, the registrar, Ms. Marcia Smith, the librarian, and her successor, Mr. Vijay Nair. Early drafts of the manuscript were typed by Mrs. Sally Kennedy, later versions by Mrs. Dorothy Swanson, secretary.

Alice Wolf Gilborn, my wife and companion, assisted with revisions and corrections. Editing someone else's work is probably near the bottom of her scale of literary preferences, but she accepted the dreary but necessary task ably and without complaint.

Harold K. Hochschild encouraged this study from the start. Author of *Township 34* and founder of the Adirondack Museum, Mr. Hochschild applied his knowledge of the region and his keen editorial eye, undimmed by his four-score-plus years, to two early drafts of the manuscript. He and his wife Mary Marquand Hochschild had wanted people to know about the distinctive Adirondack camps which were among their fondest memories of the region for many years. His satisfaction with the chapter on Camp Pine Knot was gratifying, especially since his discomfort from an injury incurred from a fall from a balky horse, in the spring of 1980, made it apparent by the following autumn that his attention, for the first time, would be concentrated on recovery and the loving company of his family and friends. Those familiar with Mr. Hochschild's book and the Adirondack Museum will readily apprehend the extent to which this book explores territory whose features were previously identified and mapped out by him.

Craig Gilborn
Adirondack Museum
Blue Mountain Lake, N.Y.

Contents

Acknowledgments v

1 Raquette Lake Hub 1

2 Land Scramble 8

3 Camp Pine Knot 19

4 Camps Cedars, Fairview, Echo 50

5 Little Forked Camp and Camp Stott 57

6 Family Matters 85

7 Ella and The Sale 89

8 Point of No Return 93

9 "The Finest Trio": Camps Uncas,
   Sagamore and Kill Kare 97

10 The Trial 132

11 Mossy Camp 137

12 William's Fall 140

13 The Later Years 144

Sources 147

Appendices 149

Index 167

Raquette Lake Hub

The Marion River Carry is a low-lying piece of land separating Utowana Lake and Raquette Lake. Along the northerly bank of the stream connecting the lakes is a broad path, formerly the bed for the abbreviated railroad which operated there between 1900 and 1929. The trail is far older, dating back to the early white settlers and probably to the first visitors, the Indians, who roamed the Adirondacks seasonally for fish, game and berries. Today the Marion River Carry is a recreational route used by persons carrying canoes, kayaks and, on occasion, Adirondack guideboats (Fig. 10), a portable rowboat, light yet strong and swift, which was an essential means of travel through a region when its roads were few and poor.

The combination of waters, mountains and forests makes the Adirondacks very nearly unique in the United States. It is possible, by alternately paddling (or rowing) and carrying a boat, to travel more than a hundred miles through the region. Roads and the automobile have dulled perceptions that once were sensitive to the natural features of the landscape. The average person in the previous century viewed the land more knowingly. An inspection of a map of the Adirondacks, for example, revealed that ownership of the highway of lakes, carries and valleys would confer control over much of the region and its future economic development. The developer's dream beckoned: Along these corridors would be carried people, freight and logs on carriages, boats and railroad trains. Dams would raise lakes and facilitate, thereby, steamboat transportation and the production of hydraulic and electrical power. Reservoirs thus created would provide guaranteed supplies of fresh water for cities as distant as New York. Hotels, summer cottages and communities would be built to accommodate transients and persons who could afford to buy second homes. These schemes seemed to assure profits to those first on the scene.

One summer day in 1876 a party of nine or ten men and women crossed the Marion River Carry path. At their backs were three lakes called the Eckford Chain; ahead, four miles to the west, lay Raquette Lake (see End Papers). Three members of the Durant family were on this outing: Dr. Thomas Clark Durant and his children, William West Durant and Heloise Hannah Durant. They and two friends, the "Misses Allen," had reached the carry by boats which met them at Eagle Lake or Blue Mountain Lake, where they had been left by Dr. Durant's carriage from North Creek.

William, years later, recalled this as his first visit to Raquette Lake. His left leg was broken and he had to be carried part of the way on the back of David Helms. Helms' brother, William, was along, together with one or two other guides. Another member, George Leavitt, was a director and surveyor for the railroad owned by Dr. Durant. He later would operate a hotel, the Forked Lake House, near the outlet of Raquette Lake.

Dr. Thomas Clark Durant, said by an admiring journalist to be an "operator," had been among the half dozen or so men who masterminded the financing and construction of the first transcontinental railroad in the United States. Vice president and manager of the Union Pacific Railroad, he commanded eighteen thousand men* at the climax of the head-

*John Todd's number, in *The Sunset Land*, Boston, 1870.

long rush to lay track from Omaha westward to a point, then unknown, where Union Pacific's rails would meet those being laid by the Central Pacific Railroad. The strain of this effort, which included being held prisoner in his railroad car by his workmen at Piedmont, Wyoming, until they received $500,000 in back pay, showed in his face and posture. He was less than fifty years old when a reporter described him as tall, neither stout nor slim, his hair and beard beginning to show streaks of gray, his face "warm, mild, thoughtful" (Fig. 1).

Heloise, called "Ella" to avoid confusing her with her mother, who had the same name, was interested in her friends and in a career as a writer or even as an actress. Her parents and brother took her seriously only when her spiritedness exceeded the narrow bounds of what they considered ladylike behavior. It was assumed that she, like her mother, would obey the men, in whose hands rested the future of the family's fortunes. The temperaments of brother and sister were alike, but William was expected some day to shoulder all the responsibilities, while her future lay in a good marriage.

Dr. Durant was something of a stranger to his family in 1876. Fifteen years earlier, having sent them off to Europe on the ship "Great Eastern," he became engrossed in plans for the Union Pacific Railroad, travelling between New York, Washington, D.C. and territories west of the Mississippi. His family lived as nomadic patricians for the next thirteen years. William attended Twickenham School in England and Bonn University in Germany, and he learned French and Italian fluently and spoke German passably well. A marble bust of him was carved in Florence by the American sculptor, Hiram Powers, when William was about thirteen (Fig. 2), a badge of membership in the ranks of wealthy Americans promenading through the capitals of Europe. Except for a reunion in 1866, when his wife and children joined him for the three day extravaganza which he planned to commemorate arrival of the railhead at the 100th meridian, Dr. Durant lived apart from his family between 1861 and 1873, a sacrifice which may have seemed justified since his work consumed most of his time. As if taking their cue from Dr. Durant, the others spent the rest of the century going separate ways and moving restlessly from one residence to another.

William and his sister were admitted to polite society in Europe. Their mother had been born in London in 1823 and there were friends and relatives with whom they stayed. William and Ella seemed suited to English society, and it is possible they betrayed mannerisms that were more British than American. A photograph taken about 1872, shortly before their return voyage to the United States (Fig. 4), reveals the fringes of the aristocratic circle in which William and Heloise moved during their sojourn abroad. According to writing on the back, Lady Richie stands to the left, Lord Napier sits on the right and three of the ladies and the two girls were later titled ("forgot their names"). William looks callow, but a sprig of flowers, probably lily-of-the-valley, is pinned to his lapel, and he wears his dark bowler hat with aplomb. Heloise sits next to her brother. In her teens but womanly nonetheless, she is bundled up in the Victorian costume of the day, as are the other ladies assembled.

On the battlefield of nineteenth century capitalism, no place for the indecisive or faint-hearted, Dr. Durant had suffered his share of setbacks. In 1867 he had been ousted as president of Crèdit Mobilier, a company which he helped form to carry on the construction and financing of the Union Pacific Railroad, of which he was vice president and manager. His removal was achieved by Oliver and Oakes Ames, manufacturers of shovels in Massachusetts, following prolonged disagreement with Dr. Durant over management. Durant remained a director of the railroad and superintended its construction until the laying of the last rail at Promontory Point on May 10, 1869 (Fig. 3), at which time the Ames brothers

2

dropped him from the directorate. He soon sold much of his Union Pacific Railroad stock, though he belonged to the railroad's board of trustees until March 11, 1874. Crèdit Mobilier stirred a national furor in 1872 when it was learned that Oakes Ames, who was a member of Congress, had with other Crèdit Mobilier men, acquired Union Pacific stock at greatly reduced cost and attempted, in 1867–68, to quash an investigation by selling stock to Congressmen. Dr. Durant testified before the Poland Committee, but he seems to have avoided being tainted by the scandal, which left Oliver Ames, who was officially condemned by the House of Representatives, a broken man. The American historian, Allan Nevins, wrote, "The consensus of historical opinion has been that Ames' action was highly improper, but that he had not contemplated bribery." Nevins observed that Ames "was a product of his time, and his ethical perceptions, like those of other business men of the day, were blunt . . . . His steps had been selfish and unethical, but not consciously corrupt." Dr. Durant and his son belonged to the same milieu.

Perhaps because of these revelations and the Panic of 1873, Dr. Durant called the family together in London that year to discuss the family's situation. Years later, his attorney traced Dr. Durant's "financial distress" in the eighties from this world-wide financial crisis. William had been in the Sudan and Ethiopia hunting, in his words, "wild beasts," and when the four gathered in London in August William presented his father with a lion cub which was soon shipped from a port in Germany to the zoo in New York City's Central Park. The zoo accepted the cub with the understanding that the Durant family would pay fifty cents a day for its food.

In April, 1874, the Durants crossed the Atlantic. William remained in New York City where he was employed for a year or two at the Equitable Loan and Trust Company which sold bonds secured by mortgages on farms in the Midwest. The others moved to a house, later called "The Gables," in North Creek, the northern terminus of Dr. Durant's railroad in the Adirondacks. Dr. Durant was busy at offices in Saratoga Springs and New York City, but life for Mrs. Durant and Ella, who were accustomed to London and Paris, must have dragged by slowly in the small town, which was the jumping-off place for people entering the Adirondack heartland from the southeast.

William would return to the Adirondacks every summer but three for the next twenty-nine years. Dr. Durant could not know this, so one imagines him, a physician turned mover of men, trying to get a measure of his son that summer day in 1876. What would be retrieved of the family's wealth and power would eventually depend on William's aptness as a pupil. His — the doctor's — glory lay in the past. As large and mysterious as the Adirondacks seemed to Easterners, nothing would compare with those years when he and a few men achieved fulfillment of a national dream across half a continent.

Father and son did not get along, which may explain why it was two years before William inspected the property on Raquette Lake. Dr. Durant, described by a family member as an "arbitrary gentleman," was not in good health, but he believed in concentrating business among family members and a small group of loyal friends and employees. Having but one son, the doctor had little choice, but neither did his son, who at twenty-six years of age knew more about spending money than making it.

We do not know the purpose of the outing. Possibly it was to inspect or choose a site for a summer camp on Long Point, not far from the inlet where the group emerged from the carry. That winter William would supervise the construction of the rustic cabins known as Camp Pine Knot. Pine Knot became famous as the first stylish camp in the Adirondacks, less a model to be copied than a quality to be captured, but it also was intended to serve as a base for furthering the Durant interests in the heart of the Adirondack wilds.

When Dr. Durant and his party reached Raquette Lake the scene was, from most vantages, unoccupied. Perhaps four year-round homes stood on its fifty or so miles of shoreline. Campsites could be seen at closer range, on several points of land and islands where guides and sportsmen had built lean-tos and rude shanties for shelter during their perennial quest for game. Members of the Constable family, of Constableville, N.Y., had camped as early as 1839 on a point known by their name, but later called Antler's Point. Over the years the trees on these desirable locations near the water had been cut for firewood or killed in the course of removing the bark for covering improvised shelters.

However, Raquette Lake and its environs had been the subject of speculative musings dating at least to the 1840's. Most of Township 40, which included nearly all of Raquette Lake, had been purchased by Farrand Benedict in 1845. Benedict, a professor at the University of Vermont, proposed building a combination railroad and steamboat line which would connect Lake Champlain, to the east, and Oneida County, a transportation and manufacturing center, to the southwest. His scheme, never carried out, is described in an appendix to *Township 34*, by Harold K. Hochschild.

In 1846, George W. Benedict, whose relationship to Farrand Benedict is not established, proposed that a canal be dug between Long Lake and Round Lake, thus diverting waters away from the upper reaches of the Raquette River into the Hudson River watershed. Work on the canal was started but never finished due to opposition from users on the Raquette downstream.

In October, 1853 the chief engineer for the Sackets Harbor & Saratoga Railroad Company, A. F. Edwards, saw the region's lakes and rivers as recreational resources, besides being avenues for tapping the interior of its forest and mineral wealth. In his *Report* to the directors of the railroad, which laid no track and was eventually to pass to Dr. Durant, he said, "Here, too, would the wealthy merchant, seeking retirement, and the amateur, delighted with the character of the place, build their ornamental cottages or country seats . . . with rustic bridges spanning the indentations of the shores . . . thus inviting varied and agreeable excursions about their transparent waters."

John Todd, a Calvinist minister in the Congregational Church, predicted that the tiny isolated community of Long Lake would eventually resemble something more like his home town of Pittsfield than a settlement in the wilderness. In his small book, *Long Lake*, published in 1845, he wrote, "This territory, when as thickly settled as Massachusetts, will contain over a million inhabitants." It followed, then, that ". . . these forests shall be cut down." Observers of the American scene fancied they saw a city rising from every crossroads hamlet encountered during their travels. But prophesies like these were derived from a combination of historical experience and an emerging technology that promised fulfillment of almost any dream. For example, John Todd was present with Dr. Durant at the ceremonial joining of the transcontinental railroad at Promontory Point in the Utah Territory, on May 10, 1869. In *The Sunset Land*, a book in which Manifest Destiny and the Gospel were blended, Reverend Todd said of the railroad, "This one road has turned the world around . . . China is our neighbor now."

More moderate views began appearing in the pages of newspapers and popular periodicals in the 1850's. The most influential of these was a four-part article published in *The New-York Daily Times* (which became *The New York Times* on September 13, 1857) by its editor, Henry Jarvis Raymond, who set forth the region's attractions for city residents. Writing in the June 19, 1855 issue, after a week's trip "through the wilderness," he said, "It may possibly be known to one in a hundred of the readers of *The Times*, that within the State of New York, and beginning within fifty miles of its capital, lies a tract of country larger than Connecticut, of as good soil as Western New York, heavily covered with as good timber as can be found in the forests of Maine, more copiously watered by beautiful lakes and streams than any other section of the United States, yet as unsettled as Nebraska, and less known than the newest state on the western borders of the American union."*

Raymond, member of a party of potential investors, was shown that "One of the most remarkable features of this wilderness is its topography, and especially the peculiar arrangement of its lakes and streams." The hub of this arterial system lay in the Raquette Lake region where the Durants would later concentrate their attentions: "Raquette Lake lies in just about the center of this [Adirondack] plateau . . . upon which, and in the vicinity of each other, rise all the principal streams of Northern and Eastern New York." Citing Ferrand Benedict, the journalist said that "Through this whole distance of about 130 miles, small boats may now be navigated, . . . and by deepening the connecting channels, and raising the water at various points by building dams, this entire chain of lakes can be made navigable for steamboats . . . ." A railroad complementing water transportation would have a predictable impact: "Its construction would immediately open the wilderness to settlement and culture, [the first effect of which] will be . . . *to raise the values of the land.*" [His emphasis.]

Thomas Clark Durant was fully aware of these exploitable natural resources when he and other investors formed the Adirondack Company in 1863. Its predecessor, The Sackets Harbor and Saratoga Railroad Company, as Raymond observed in 1855, was "owner of 500,000 acres of land [that] has cost them virtually nothing." By 1871 Dr. Durant's railroad ended in North Creek, about forty-five miles from Raquette Lake, so it was necessary to open a line of stagecoaches to Blue Mountain Lake and carry travellers and freight from there to Raquette Lake by boat.

Raquette Lake was crucial to Dr. Durant's aim of controlling the central portion of the Adirondack region, since it was his ultimate goal, never fulfilled by him or his son, to see the railroad extended 170 miles northward to Canada through undeveloped lands largely under his control. The configuration of rivers and lakes resembles the letter Y lying to the right, on its long side, with Raquette Lake at the junction. Running westward from there to Old Forge is the Fulton Chain of Lakes. East of Raquette Lake is the Eckford Chain of Lakes, which, with the addition of Dr. Durant's stages, extended the line eastward to North Creek. The richest territory, however, lay along the northeasterly diagonal described by the Raquette River. The Raquette River, in reality a succession of lakes and rivers, constituted a vital artery which supplied and opened up the region around Tupper Lake and the Saranac Lakes miles to the north.

In 1886 William was quoted in a story published in the *New York Daily Tribune.* "I firmly believe," he said, "that the Adirondacks are the resort of the future." His plans, he said, called for an elaborate system of stagecoaches and steamboats that would move tourists through the northerly axis formed by the Raquette River and Long Lake. Part of the system — the steamboats on Raquette Lake and Long Lake — was already in place, he added, but he did not mention that his steamboat *Buttercup* has been sent to the bottom of Long Lake by a resident who resented this mechanized encroachment on the services of guides and their guideboats.

---

*Similarities may be discerned in a remark written twelve years earlier by John Todd, who should be given his due:

"The fact is new and seems strange to many that there should be in the North Eastern part of New York a wilderness almost unbroken and unexplored, embracing a territory larger than the whole state of Massachusetts."

5

When Dr. Webb's trans-Adirondack railroad became a reality in 1892, William included it in the earlier plans. A spur would take travellers by train from the north end of Raquette Lake to the landing at the inlet of Long Lake (End Papers). A steamboat would carry them eighteen or so miles to the outlet, at which point they would climb on another train that passed between Tupper and Saranac Lake, joining the main line of the railroad built by Dr. Webb. As late as 1900, William would express partial support for the construction of reservoirs on the Raquette River. It might, he said, "help to get good navigation down through Long Lake to Saranac." Some of William's lands, including 4,000 acres on Upper Saranac Lake, were located in this region north of Long Lake.

It was not by chance, then, that Dr. Durant and his son concentrated their attentions on the development of land near Raquette Lake and in the tracts immediately surrounding the lake and the township of which it was a part. Anything going into or coming out of the central Adirondacks — people, freight, logs, even water — was to a great degree affected by what happened on and around Raquette Lake.

Dr. Durant's ability to develop his Adirondack holdings was obvious to all who knew him. A masterly promoter and salesman, he mounted one of frontier America's grandest events in the fall of 1866 when several hundred well-connected guests, many from the East, were taken by steamboat and rail to Omaha in a scheme to raise money and support for the Union Pacific Railroad. Entertained there at a banquet and ball, the group merrily boarded a nine-car excursion train which carried them to the 100th meridian longitude, about 247 miles distant, the furthest point then reached by Durant's tracks. Dr. Durant's family and closest friends occupied the private car in which President Lincoln's body had been borne to Springfield, Illinois, the year before. The invitees, prominent in politics and business, used comfortably furnished tents and were regaled for three days by a series of events deemed appropriate to the frontier setting. There was an Indian war dance, followed that evening by a mock raid on the camp. The second and third days witnessed vaudeville acts, a band concert, a demonstration of track laying by Irish laborers, and a battle between Indians. On the return trip to Omaha, at nightfall, they watched in awe as the train approached a grass fire which had been set by Durant's workmen on a 20-mile stretch of prairie.

Dr. Durant also promoted the Adirondacks. A glowing editorial about the Adirondacks was printed in the August 9, 1864, issue of *The New York Times*. It mentioned the start of Dr. Durant's railroad, which, the writer said, promised a true union between utility and enjoyment. In a phrase as startlingly fresh today as it was then, the editor saw the Adirondacks as a country "fitted to make a Central Park for the world," soon to be accessible by rail to people from all walks of life. Dr. Durant reprinted the editorial in a pamphlet issued by his railroad during its construction between Saratoga Springs and North Creek.

Possibly Durant had a role in supplying information to C. M. Hoppin, the author of an article in the March, 1869, issue of the English periodical, *Broadway Magazine*. It requires, Hoppin said, "no prophet to predict that in twenty years, all along the shores of the Racket [sic] River and Long Lake, and Racket Lake, the cheerful farm-houses, or even the summer residences of the wealthy, will be seen."

Dr. Durant investigated the publication of a book on the Adirondacks. He consulted with Edmund C. Steadman (1833–1908), a broker and literary figure in New York, who replied by saying that he could not write it but that his, Steadman's, outline combined an "attractive & valuable" survey for the general reader, while at the same time "bringing everything to bear on the necessities for, *condition & golden prospects of your enterprise.*" [His emphasis.] Continuing, Steadman said "Plenty of books have been written on the

6

Adirondacks, but I suppose the special object of this one is to interest people in the fact that this rich region is being *opened* to New York & Boston, &c., and to embrace in more systematic order all the statistics & attractions of the tract, & of your Company." Dr. Durant knew well enough that there would be no buyers of his land without a system of transportation to give them access to it, and that once the system was in place it was necessary to advertise its services. He succeeded, though not until the year after his death, for in 1886 appeared the first of four seasonal travel guides published by the Adirondack Railway Company. Its cover printed in imitation of birch bark, the series was entitled *Birch Bark from the Adirondacks; Or, From City to Trail*, each volume containing maps, woodcut illustrations, timetables, advertisements and a narrative by Frank H. Taylor reassuring the reader of the ease and security of travel through the region served by the railroad and its connecting stagecoach and steamboat lines. Edward Bierstadt's books of photographs of places and scenes in the Adirondacks, published about 1886 and described elsewhere in these pages, was another venture in which Dr. Durant almost surely had a hand.

Land Scramble 2

What flour is to the baker, land was to the Durants and men like them. It took money, political influence and the marshalling of vast human resources to establish a civilization on the abundant but unsettled lands of the American West. In 1869 Dr. Durant told a reporter with simple finality, "I had built roads before over the prairies in advance of settlements, and I knew how they bring population and make business from the very outset."

In the New World there was nothing new to this. Monarchs in England made grants of vast tracts to colonial companies and such individuals as Lord Baltimore and William Penn. Expansion of industry, trade and imperial power were considered far more important to the "commonwealth" in the long run than the personal advantages and abuses that might ensue in the short term. In this spirit the U.S. Congress amended the charter of the Union Pacific Company, doubling its land grant to the company and making the company's mortgage bonds a first-lien on the railroad. The chief architect of that revision, which occurred in the winter of 1863–64, was Thomas Clark Durant. In the same spirit, the backers of a railroad through the Adirondacks went to the legislature and Governor in 1870 for a state subsidy of $1.7 million toward the $5.5 million for extending the track to Ogdensburg, on the St. Lawrence River. George M. Gleason, an Assemblyman through whose district the road was to run, addressed the Assembly on March 29 with urgency still heard in Albany on North Country matters. Citing infusions of state money elsewhere, he said his constituents "are tired of waiting," and that "this is a case like the great Pacific railroad, where the improvement must *precede* the population instead of *follow* it." Leading the current effort, he said, was Dr. Thomas C. Durant, "the man who, by his indomitable energy, will and perseverance, and by his great executive ability, secured the construction of the Union Pacific Railroad." The measure passed the Assembly and Senate but was vetoed by Governor Hoffman in April because the legislature failed to indicate its preference among six other bills for aid elsewhere in New York.

Dr. Durant had been born in 1820 in Lee, Massachusetts, not many miles distant from the Albany Medical College from which he was graduated twenty years later. He practiced medicine for three years, and would later regret not having pursued his interest in "natural science." In April, 1870, he gave the college $15,000 for the establishment of a professorship of surgery in memory of Dr. Alden March, a former teacher.

About 1843, he and a younger brother, Charles Wright Durant (1821–1885), became partners in a grain shipping firm, soon known as Durant, Lathrop & Company, which had been started by their uncles. The young physician-turned-businessman ran the branch office in New York City, from which grain was shipped to many of the principal ports of Europe. He successfully speculated in stocks and gradually, with Charles, turned his attention to transportation in the American West, where the firm was sending merchandise as well as grain and flour.

By the age of 31 he had embarked on a career in railroading, having been joined by a third brother, William Franklin Durant (1823–1899), in holding interests in several midwestern railroads. The three men were connected with the Chicago and Rock Island Railroad, of which Charles was the president for many years. William was a contractor for the Rock Island road across Iowa and he was one of the contractors for the Union Pacific Railroad. William spent his last thirty years in Chicago, while Thomas and Charles resided in Brooklyn and New York City.

Dr. Durant was a railroad builder when he turned his attention to the transcontinental railroad. It was about then, in 1861, that he sent his wife, Heloise Hannah Timbrell Durant, and two children to Europe. Mrs. Durant had been born in England, where her father kept a shop and gave lessons on the violin. She and Thomas were married in Little Rock, Arkansas, in 1847.

At the time that Dr. Durant was engineering the financing of the transcontinental railroad, he or others were negotiating the purchase of property controlled by the Adirondack Estate and Railroad Company. This company had been incorporated on April 10, 1848 as the Sackets Harbor and Saratoga Railroad Company. Under reorganization in 1857, it became the Lake Ontario and Hudson River Railroad Company.

The laws passed by New York State affecting this and other railroads granted a number of concessions which can only be described as generous. For example, the 1848 act incorporating the Sackets Harbor and Saratoga road allowed the owners to select and purchase any quantity of land belonging to the state in Herkimer and Hamilton Counties, up to 250,000 acres, for a nickel an acre. The company was empowered to raise operating money by selling, leasing and mortgaging any lands purchased from the state or individuals. Construction was to begin within three years; the track, to run between Saratoga Springs and Sackets Harbor, was to be laid within ten years.

A more liberal law was passed in 1850. It permitted railroad companies to condemn land, authorized the commissioners of the Land Office to grant lands belonging to the state, and gave surveyors the right to enter onto all lands without hindrance. Dr. Durant entered the scene under a law passed in 1862 permitting the purchaser of what by then was called the Lake Ontario and Hudson Railroad Company to form a new company for completing the railroad. The new company was the Adirondack Company. It was authorized to use "products of the forests," to extract iron and transport it and logs. Within 4½ years the company's track was supposed to extend from Saratoga Springs or Ballston Spa to the southern border of the Essex County line. On April 27, 1863, another act was passed which exempted the Adirondack Company's lands, up to 1 million acres, from taxation until September 12, 1883. Excepted from this exemption were lands on which improvements, such as road beds, were to be made.

The Adirondack Company was the only railroad to fulfill part of the "bargain" made with the state in 1848 and the years that followed. Construction started in 1864 and by December 1, 1865 it boasted 25 miles of track. After a delay of two years, 12 miles of track were laid in 1868, 12 more in 1869 and 11 in 1870. The cost, according to the company, came to $3,000,000 by 1870, in which year it announced net earnings of $45,736.62. Much of Dr. Durant's Union Pacific money must have been invested in the Adirondack Company's railroad, which a reporter called the doctor's "plaything of a railway in the Adirondacks." The track extended as far as North River, though its real terminus was in North Creek, several miles below this point. By 1870 the westward route to Sackets Harbor on Lake Ontario had been dropped in favor of a more northerly route to Ogdensburg, 125 miles above the North Creek terminus (Fig. 5). This extension would never be built, though Dr. Durant actively looked for investors in England between 1869 and 1874, and he and his associates attempted, as mentioned, to obtain a subsidy from the state in 1870 that would have made it far easier for them to obtain additional capital in New York City and London.

In exchange for the sixty mile railroad, Dr. Durant, through the Adirondack Company, secured control of vast tracts of land which had been acquired at little cost from the state and which were, for the most part, exempt from taxation until 1883. The exact acreage is not known. The company's prospectus of 1863 said the "estate" was two million acres, a figure that Harold K. Hochschild finds excessive. In 1872 the company claimed ownership of 540,000 acres, with options to another 100,000 acres. Years later, William West Durant recalled that the company's holdings totalled 658,261 acres in seven counties, though he did not give a date or say whether this quantity was the most ever held by the Adirondack Company or its successor firm, also in Durant hands, the Adirondack Railway Company.

The property was a potential rather than an immediate source of wealth. The railroad was but one of several opportunities for development: The timber could be sold apart from the land, and minerals under the land, chiefly iron-bearing ore, could be extracted by the company and shipped on its railroad. Cleared lands could be sold for agricultural purposes and they could be divided and then sold for recreational development. Land was also a medium of exchange for cash or services. By the Adirondack Company's own estimate, of about 1871, only about one-quarter of its 540,000 acres were for railroad purposes. The remaining 400,000 acres were for other purposes, such as timber, iron mining and agriculture.

The drawback of land was that it could not be readily turned into hard cash, titles to it were often of questionable validity, and development schemes were notoriously subject to vagaries of the national economy. It was also subject to taxation. The Durants were land rich and, to an uncertain degree, money poor. But from Dr. Durant's vantage point, the Adirondack region was ripe for development, for surrounding it were dozens of cities with soaring populations aspiring for a place to spend the summer and hungry for the other resources which the Adirondacks possessed in abundance — timber, water, minerals and the land itself.

America and Britain were at war when New York State appropriated an estimated 7 million acres of land belonging to the British Crown. In 1792 slightly more than half of these lands were sold to Alexander Macomb for about eight cents an acre. The state referred to the property as "waste and unappropriated," thereby rationalizing the shedding of state lands in the Adirondacks to private buyers until state policy began to be reversed in the 1870's.

How much New York had relinquished is indicated in a report issued in 1872 by the newly created Park Commission. Of the approximately 2 million acres that comprised the wild heart of the Adirondack region, all or most of it formerly owned by the state, less than 40,000 acres still belonged to New York. The reversal of state practice was manifest in the decades that followed, so that today New York owns nearly 2½ million acres in what is called the Adirondack Park. Even so, its holdings make up only about 40% of all the lands in the Park.

By 1870, Dr. Thomas Clark Durant owned or controlled far more land in the Adirondacks than did New York. All or most of the Adirondack Company's land had been sold by New York, which regarded the isolated region as an outsized wilderness resistant to taming. The land was unsuitable for farming, and transportation through the region was costly and difficult. The majority of Americans skirted the Adirondack uplands in their trek to find better lives to the west. Partly for reasons of personal greed and partly because of a desire to stimulate economic development, successive legislatures and administrations in Albany before the Civil War sanctioned the selling of Adirondack lands which were seen to be unproductive until they passed into private hands and generated income from taxes.

Before mid-century a pattern had developed whereby large tracts sold to speculators like Macomb were divided and sold to lumbering interests which cut the timber and allowed the denuded land to return to the state for unpaid taxes. The lands in default were sold at tax sales and the stage was set for resumption of the cycle. The process is described by Norman Van Valkenburgh in *The Adirondack Forest Preserve*, a study issued in 1969 and republished in book form by the Adirondack Museum in 1979.

Keeping up payments of taxes on Adirondack holdings proved difficult for people who inherited large tracts or acquired them cheaply for later profit. In 1885 the legislature passed a law which detailed the steps by which lands were to be sold for unpaid taxes. If taxes and interest were unpaid for two years, the state comptroller placed the delinquent property up for sale following a notification period of ten weeks. A buyer, upon paying the taxes and interest, received a certificate of purchase. However, the original owner had a two-year grace period in which to reclaim his land, being required to pay an additional ten percent interest per year to the holder of the certificate. If the original owner did not redeem the property, the comptroller conveyed a tax title to the tax sale purchaser.

Buying and selling Adirondack lands was a thriving business in the nineteenth century. A handful of men, Dr. Durant and his son among them, were adept at it, using land as a medium of exchange or holding it for its potential for lumber or development as a summer resort. Occasionally taxes were withheld deliberately as a stratagem for obtaining a tax title to lands whose titles were "clouded" and therefore insecure.

Most of the Durant family's lands enjoyed an exemption from taxation dating from 1863: this privilege, an inducement for constructing a railroad through the Adirondacks, expired in 1883. The Durants, hard pressed thereafter to pay their taxes, joined the rush to Albany to pay back taxes before a tax sale or expiration of the grace period for redemption. "Get the cancellation of taxes along as fast as you can," growled Dr. Durant in a terse letter to his son on March 8, 1885.

*   *   *

The opening of Raquette Lake as a resort began with the construction of Camp Pine Knot during the winter of 1876–77. Over the next thirty years, many camps and hotels were erected on Raquette Lake and neighboring lakes. Much of this activity was due to Dr. Thomas Clark Durant and his son William. They acquired land in the region and assisted friends and other members of the Durant family in doing the same. They supervised the construction of summer camps, built and improved roads, dug channels and built dams between lakes for steamboat traffic, operated saw mills, installed a telegraph line from Saratoga Springs to Blue Mountain Lake, raised money and gave land for building churches, and set up a stagecoach line between Blue Mountain Lake and North Creek (Fig. 30). They encouraged the opening of resort hotels on Blue Mountain and Raquette Lakes.

The Durant family's early plans depended on the availability of land in Township 40, in which Raquette Lake was located. This posed no problem as long as the state continued its practice of disposing of land at tax sales and allowing the occupants of existing camps to lease and buy lands to which the state might lay a claim. But the state, in response to public criticism of its laxity, began reserving lands for itself at periodic tax sales held in Albany. Most of Township 40 was peremptorily set aside by the state to itself at tax sales in 1871, 1877 and 1881.

Dr. Durant attended the 1877 sale. His lawyer, George Fowler, got into a "chewing match" with an official of the state when 19,435 acres, most of the township, were removed from public bidding. Durant's lawyer asserted that the state had no right to build title to itself on tax delinquent lands by excluding private parties from the bidding.

Dr. Durant's objections had a legal basis, for the courts later invalidated the tax sale of 1871 because the supervisors for Hamilton County had failed to verify the tax roles for the years 1863 through 1865. This, the courts said, rendered the tax sales invalid, and it nullified the titles claimed by the state through them. A "curative act" passed by the legislature in 1885, in which the state tried to clear titles acquired by it through tax sales, did not apply to invalid titles acquired prior to the act. The state's titles were thus no better than claimants who could trace occupancy to a tract prior to 1871. In a case decided in 1910, the judge said that "Where legal title is established by neither party . . ., the one showing prior possession in himself or in those through whom he claims, although for a period less than that which is requisite to confer a title by adverse possession, will be deemed to have the better right."

Even so, the state retained its ownership of almost all of Township 40. Starting about 1897, it took legal action to eject the occupants of several tracts on the lake. As suggested by the judgment quoted in part above, the state was unsuccessful in establishing its claims to most of the contested properties, but the years of judgment, appeal and counter-action exposed a flawed substructure of land ownership in the township.

Dr. Durant's failure to acquire more than a few hundred acres of land in Township 40 was a serious blow to his plans. He and his son would own extensive tracts in townships adjacent to this one. But the emergence of the state as a buyer rather than a seller of Adirondack land introduced a new player and uncertainty to the game of land speculation in the Adirondacks.

Township 40 is very likely the most litigated township in the Adirondacks. The state lost its suits more often than not — in fact, New York may not have won a single action in the township in which the defendant had money and fortitude to carry his case to a higher court. The legal tangle was largely due to the uncertain validity of titles traceable to the early residents on the lake. Osprey Island is a model of sorts for understanding the confused state of affairs that existed elsewhere on the lake.

The seventeen acre island had been occupied in 1868 by William "Adirondack" Murray, a lecturer and author of the popular guide to the Adirondacks, *Adventures in the Wilderness*. The next year, when the book was published, Murray shared his shanty with Alvah Dunning, a trapper, hunter and guide who had built a camp on the western shore of the lake and another on Eighth Lake, a few miles to the southwest. Dunning later said that Murray gave the island to him.

The Durant family tried quietly to gain custodianship of the island, but nothing came of these efforts until 1879, when William West Durant submitted an application on behalf of his cousin, Charles W. Durant, Jr. The application said that Osprey Island had become cut and burned over by temporary camping parties "who had no interest in its preservation." The Land Office in Albany designated Charles as "custodian," a term which the report of 1886 by the Forest Commission, successor to the Land Office, said had never been defined, adding, "nor does it appear what rights the custodian gains by his appointment." Charles asked that he be permitted to buy the island in 1879 but no action was taken on his request.

Charles hired four men to clear brush on the island for a camp, but Alvah Dunning threatened them with an axe or gun as they approached and they retreated in their boat. In

12

1880 the standoff of the previous summer was resolved when Mrs. Thomas Clark Durant, who lived at Camp Pine Knot about a mile away, gently talked Dunning into vacating his shanty and the island for one hundred dollars. The next year he received a similar sum for signing a deed which turned Osprey Island over to Charles W. Durant, Jr.* This deed was not recorded until May 6, 1891, when the rustic camp and its island were sold to Joseph H. Ladew, a leather merchant from New York City.

On September 1, 1897, the state initiated an action to eject the Ladews. A seesaw court struggle ensued with a referee finding in the state's favor about 1901, followed by a reversal in the Court of Appeals in 1907. The state, pressing its case, perhaps on other grounds, won another decision on October 25, 1915. The case was being argued in 1920 when evidence and earlier testimony was presented in anticipation of further appeal by Ladew. A new trial was ordered but Ladew and the state settled and the Attorney General dismissed the state's action.

The state's argument was that the "People of the State" had taken possession of Osprey Island (and its tiny neighbor) when the Land Board designated Charles as custodian of the island in 1879. However, Ladew claimed title through Dunning's occupancy, which not only pre-dated Charles's custodianship but also the tax sale of 1871. That sale had been invalidated and tax deeds possessed by the state from that and subsequent sales were unenforceable, according to a decision made in 1910 in favor of Horace Inman, the occupant of another island on Raquette Lake.

The law provided for ownership by "adverse possession," and much of the testimony given in the Ladew case was used by the attorneys for both sides to show the nature of Dunning's occupancy of the island. Was his shanty (Fig. 38) a "permanent improvement" as required by the ancient legal custom of squatter's right? The state was skeptical, but a dozen or so long-time residents, whose recollections stretched back to the 1860s, indicated that Dunning spent much time on the island and that, however modest, his shanty was his home.

In the 1880's and early '90's New York officials expressed sympathy for people who had erected cottages on land claimed by the state. A camp was started for Frank H. Stott on Bluff Point in 1878 on state land. In 1884 a special act was approved by the legislature permitting the commissioners of the Land Office to lease up to 160 acres of land to Stott for thirty years at $20 a year. The hand of Dr. Durant and his son, who married Stott's daughter that year, may be discerned in this and several other efforts to acquire land on which camps had already been constructed on Raquette Lake. The wording of the special act for Stott, dated June 6, 1884, reflected the state's solicitude. The act said that the Bluff Point tract may be leased and observed, ". . . upon which [land], in contemplation of purchase, he has erected permanent improvements," an acknowledgment from the legislature itself which gave the Stott family a certain proprietary claim to the property in the future.

Frank Stott, a textile manufacturer, faithfully paid the annual fee into the 1890's. As described in Chapter 5, the camp was enlarged during this period. The Stotts eventually obtained title to the land, for the property was sold by the family for $20,000 on May 31, 1910 to Robert J. Collier, the magazine publisher.

Efforts to wrest ownership of the township from the state continued despite the tax sales of 1871 and 1877. On December 20, 1881, two men, "Eherhardt and Cotterill," applied to the Land Office for the purchase of most of Township 40. A renewal of the application was made on January 31, 1883. The board did not act, except to order a survey

*In May, 1899, Alvah held out for — and got — $600 for his property on the western shore of the lake, needed by the Raquette Lake Railway for a terminal site. The railroad also got his shanty, furniture and three boats.

to be made; however, it authorized the Land Office to sell the township to the two parties and it also allowed the state to sell up to 160 acres of land to each person occupying "improved" land on Raquette Lake. The Durants may have been working behind the scene on this matter. In 1900 William West Durant wrote a letter to one "J. H. Ehrehart" of Hoboken, N.J. concerning a land survey.

Charles Durant was unsuccessful in his efforts to purchase Osprey Island. His applications were turned down on May 3 and December 5, 1882, and special acts on his behalf languished in the legislature in 1884 and 1885. The uncertainty of his claim probably explains the sporadic progress in the construction of Camp Fairview during the period 1880 to 1885.

The flurry of activity to establish claims on Raquette Lake in 1879–1885 was spurred by proposals in Albany which would curtail the freedom with which the state disposed of its Adirondack holdings. A report of 1886 said that the state did not know how much land it owned and, citing long-existing abuses, called for a new survey before the Adirondack region was "further reduced by eager squatters and land-stealers who have for so long a time regarded the state . . . merely as a goose to be plucked."

In 1883 the legislature passed a law prohibiting the sale of state lands in the ten Adirondack counties. Two other laws provided $10,000 for the purchase of lands in those counties and assigned Verplanck Colvin to undertake a survey of state lands. In 1885 a law was approved which established the Forest Preserve and created a three-man Forest Commission to replace the Land Office. It reiterated the ban on land sales and added another which prohibited the leasing of land in the Forest Preserve. These measures marked the beginning of the end of easy land grabbing in the Adirondacks.

Dr. Durant and his son were nothing if not resourceful and undoubtedly they were among the backers of an act which was passed in 1887 allowing the state to sell or exchange "separate small tracts" of state land. This undid much of the intent of earlier laws. Approval of the "Forever Wild" provision to the Constitution in 1894, which prohibited the sale and leasing of Forest Preserve lands and the removal of timber from such lands, was pooh-poohed and even subverted by a variety of persons who believed that economic necessity would soon overcome the "sentimental opposition" to timber and railroad development in the Adirondacks. The state's resolve, bolstered by experience in conservation and its administration, growing public support and precedent in judicial decisions, eventually eliminated most attempts to gain a foothold on Forest Preserve lands for personal gain.

The Durants lost the big prize — Township 40 — but they won some small ones in Township 40. Osprey Island is privately owned, though Camp Fairview no longer stands on it. Other parcels directly or indirectly associated with the Durant family are also in private hands under the principle of early occupancy. Ownership of land at little or no initial cost was obtained through two routes. One leased land, built a camp on it and then tried to buy the land, or, if the land could not be purchased, one tried to enter a claim to it by "adverse possession," a squatter's claim, which pointed up the importance of obtaining deeds or evidence traceable back to the earliest residents on the lake.

Fig. 1   The strain of building the Union Pacific Railroad shows in Dr. Thomas Clark Durant's face in a photograph taken about 1869. He was 49 at the time and was soon to turn his
full attention to developing his properties in the Adirondacks. Adirondack Museum.

Fig. 2   This is one of several photographs taken of William West Durant at a studio in Florence, Italy when a boy of about twelve. His mother and sister also lived abroad while Dr. Durant built the transcontinental railroad. Adirondack Museum.

Fig. 3 & 3A   A. J. Russell took this picture on May 10, 1869 at Promontory Point in the Utah Territory, where the joining of the tracks of the Union Pacific and Central Pacific Railroads linked the Atlantic and Pacific Oceans, signalling the start of a national celebration. Dr. Durant, a chief figure for the project's eastern end, is shown in the detail (below) (Fig. 3A), with Rev. John Todd to his left. Heloise, the doctor's daughter, who was sixteen in 1869, may be shown to the right, as comparison with Fig. 4 suggests. Photo courtesy of The Oakland Museum.

Fig. 4   *William and his sister Heloise are seated on a bench to the left in this photograph of an outing in England about 1871. The others were identified on the back of the original as members of the British aristocracy. Lord Napier is to the right. Adirondack Museum, gift of Mrs. Bromley Seeley.*

Camp Pine Knot 3

Until 1876 William West Durant had never been in the Adirondacks. A traveller in England, Europe and Africa for about eleven years, he brought an unjaded eye to the shanties that he encountered during his first visits to Raquette Lake. Three of these belonged to Alvah Dunning, who used them as combination homes, guest houses and outposts for his several occupations as guide, trapper and carpenter. Durant's newness to the region and to roughly built shelters like Dunning's on Osprey Island is evident in testimony he gave nearly forty years later, in 1915. "As I recollect, it was a low roofed camp, I had never seen anything like it before, for I had never been in this country before, or any kind of country like this; and, as I recollect it, there was some bark on it and I think some boards. . . ." An early photograph (Fig. 38), taken about 1873, shows a simple-gable shanty, nine to ten feet high at the ridge with walls and roof covered with sheets of spruce bark. Rocks hold the bark to the roof, from which a stove-pipe protrudes.

It would be too easy to conclude that William's first Adirondack experiences were the source of the rustic aesthetic that evolved under his tutelage in subsequent years, but circumstances in 1876 surely contributed to the appropriateness of building with locally available materials and skills. The garden houses, bridges, fences and other "factitious accompaniments" judiciously placed for effect in parks and gardens of estates in England and Europe were certainly familiar to Durant, who attended school in Twickenham, where Alexander Pope had fashioned one of Europe's first picturesque gardens 150 years earlier. Closer to home were examples of rustic work in Central Park (1859 and after) in New York City and Brooklyn's Prospect Park (1866), the latter partly on land purchased from William's mother in 1869. In the city or its fringes, rustic work was an adornment to the park, which was itself a "natural" accessory to the cityscape. In the Adirondacks rustic materials were an eminently practical solution to the problem of shelter — cheap, near at hand, serviceable and, to the eyes of a newly transplanted cosmopolitan like Durant, rich with its suggestive power to charm men and women accustomed to parlors and counting rooms in the city.

Camp Pine Knot was the first of William West Durant's camps, and it remains, in its comparatively smaller scale and rustic detailing, perhaps the finest of the grand camps that were erected under his supervision in the Adirondacks between 1876 and 1901. The novelty of Pine Knot was first discerned, in print, by the photographer and publisher of travel guides, Seneca Ray Stoddard (1844–1917), of Glens Falls. In the 1881 edition of *The Adirondacks, Illustrated*, Stoddard said the camp was "unquestionably the most picturesque and *recherché* affair of its kind in the wilderness." By 1888 he had traversed the region sufficiently to say, "The pioneer camp of this section, and one of the most artistic in the woods, is Camp Pine Knot." Camps like Pine Knot, he added, are "never completed *really*," being "bound by no rule of time or architecture" and "never exactly the same one year [as] the year before." Easily the most important and prolific photographer of the Adirondack scene before World War I, Stoddard had reason to praise Pine Knot, since he worked for the Durants more than once before 1899 and both he and the Durants labored to lure business to the Adirondacks. But his appraisal was accurate and stood the test of time.

The historian Alfred L. Donaldson, who quizzed William while preparing the two-volume work, *A History of the Adirondacks*, published in 1921, said that Durant, in combining the features of the log cabin with those of the Swiss chalet at Pine Knot, achieved the start of "a distinctive school of Adirondack architecture," the "prototype of the modern Camp Beautiful." Donaldson saw that Pine Knot was a source of inspiration, not of imitation: "Before it was built there was nothing like it; since then, despite infinite variations, there has been nothing essentially different from it." Durant's contribution conjured a distinctive life style in the woods. "He was the first," Donaldson wrote, "to make his summer quarters comfortable for winter pleasures and to use them for that purpose. He was the first to ask his friends to travel north by train and then by sleigh over forty miles of snow and ice for the novelty of eating Christmas dinner in the wilderness. He was, in short, the first to inaugurate many things which had never been dreamed of in the Adirondacks before."

In looking at Camp Pine Knot, which today is the Outdoor Education Center of the State University of New York College at Cortland, it is important to note that the complex of ten cottages and some dozen or so other structures represented, by the time of their sale to Collis P. Huntington in 1895, the accumulated labor and refinement of twenty years of living and experimentation. In addition, there were other camps on Raquette Lake and nearby lakes which were scarcely less sophisticated than Pine Knot, which was intended by Dr. Durant and his son to be a showplace for enticing investors and tourists to the region. These other camps were probably more completely developed by 1889 than Pine Knot. Finally, William West Durant was the moving genius behind the development of Donaldson's "Camp Beautiful," but the men who worked for him, familiar as they were with the uses of timber and bark for shelter, deserve a measure of credit for implementing Durant's ideas, or rather the effects Durant wanted and insisted upon. These men, most of them jacks-of-all-trade with a specialty of carpentry, moved from camp to camp, taking their skills and experiences with them.

At least three professional photographers recorded Camp Pine Knot between 1877 and 1895: Seneca Ray Stoddard, Edward Bierstadt and Alonzo Mix. Their photographs, with additional documents, allow one to trace the evolution of the camp during its ownership by the Durants and Collis P. Huntington.

The first period, 1876–78, includes William's first visit and the construction, in the winter of 1876–77, of a one-story chalet, a one-room log cabin or two, an open dining room, kitchen building, and platforms for two tents (Figs. 39, 41). The site chosen, on a neck of land on the south shore of Long Point, had been acquired by Dr. Durant from Charlie Bennett in exchange for the doctor's services in obtaining land titles for Bennett in Albany. According to Harold K. Hochschild in *Township 34*, Dr. Durant had owned a tract on the north side of Long Point on which several cabins were built, but this site was discarded for the sunnier location on the south shore, a half mile distant. The chalet nodded perfunctorily to the Swiss style, which was not yet in vogue in the U.S., but the cottage owed as much to ramshackle construction like that at Alvah Dunning's camp on Osprey Island as to Central Europe. Improvisation and roughness characterized Pine Knot in its first few years.

The second stage of construction opened in 1879 when William altered or removed some of the buildings, principally the chalet, which was supplanted by about 1882 by what

20

he later called a "Swiss Cottage," a two-story structure containing a large living room and four bedrooms (**Fig. 44**). Structural evidence — log construction on the first floor and frame construction for the second — suggests that part of the original building may have been incorporated into the new one. The Swiss Cottage became the focal point of the complex of buildings at Pine Knot. Still standing, it asserted in size, regularity and stylistic pretentions its role as headquarters for the Durant family in the central Adirondacks.

By 1888 Pine Knot had emerged in its rustic glory, perhaps just short of what a historian might call a "golden age" of development. Landscaping, an unexamined aspect of William's camps, is evident in the lawns and ample footpaths between cottages (**Fig. 46**). Rustic planters, window boxes and tree stumps contained plants, ferns and flowers; and vines grew luxuriantly up the porches of several cottages. Glass-enclosed kerosene lanterns were placed every so many feet to illuminate paths between buildings, cheerful beacons for travellers on the lake. One departing visitor said, "The effect of the camp fire was very much increased by colored lights put about in various directions and let off as we steamed away — a beautiful picture always to remember." Two tents, one gaily striped, were shown in an 1888 photograph, an indication that tents continued to be used after they had ceased to be an absolute necessity. The stonework that became a signature of William West Durant's camps was in evidence at this time; stove pipes had been replaced by chimneys of brick and quarried native stone.

An unusual amenity at Camp Pine Knot was the floating camp built for the Durants by 1878. An ink drawing in the guest book that year shows boys and girls swimming and fishing from a raft of logs to which a cabin had been attached (**Fig. 6**). William replaced the raft some years later with what Donaldson called "an elaborate scow houseboat." Beached at Pine Knot today, the cabin of this later houseboat was sheathed with cedar bark on the outside and contained two bedrooms, a kitchen and two small baths. The interior was paneled with boards of southern pine. The houseboat, called the "Barque of Pine Knot," was towed by a launch to any place on the lake that suited William's fancy (**Fig. 43**). Four could sleep on it away from distractions at camp; it also afforded partial relief from black flies and mosquitoes, which were more prevalent over land than water. The artist A. F. Tait had a raft which he used as a floating studio on Long Lake earlier in the century, so William was not the first to introduce the houseboat to the Adirondacks.

The third and single most extensive construction phase occurred about 1889–1892, a period when William, flush with money from the sale of the Adirondack Railway Company, also commissioned the building of an ocean-going yacht in Philadelphia. To the cottage usually reserved for Mrs. T. C. Durant, William attached a bedroom, dressing room, stove room and bathroom. To this he added a rambling "Annex" (**Fig. 50**) which contained rooms for his children and a governess. A covered walkway from the nursery to a summer house may have been built at this time. The Durant Cottage was built during this period (**Fig. 47**). It contained three rooms, a bath and two fireplaces, and it summarized William's current thought about rustic design and detailing, both outside and within.

In August, 1890, the wealthy industrialist, Collis P. Huntington, stayed at Pine Knot with his wife. The enlargement of the camp in 1889–1892 may have partly been due to William's courtship of Huntington, who purchased the camp with its many buildings, furnishings and 200 acres in the spring of 1895.

Huntington was a regular visitor to Pine Knot between 1895 and 1900, usually in August. He corresponded with John E. Tillson, the caretaker whom William had found, from the Southern Pacific Company's offices in New York City, where he worked and lived when not on business in San Francisco. William assisted in the management of Pine Knot, a service which Huntington rewarded by allowing himself to be used for William's purposes when self-interest permitted it.

Three extant buildings are found at Pine Knot that cannot be accounted for in William's fifteen-page inventory of 1895. Since Pine Knot was unoccupied by the Huntington family after 1900 (except for caretakers), we can assume that these buildings were erected between 1895 and 1900, the fourth and last phase in the camp's formative history. Durant's role in them is uncertain, but the reliance on stone, bark and poles was continued. The buildings are known today by the Outdoor Education Center as the Staff House, Dormitory and Recreation Hall. The last was the most spectacular, with the gabled ends of the porch and pavillion roofs, one over the other, worked out with rustic filigree and sunburst patterns (Fig. 51). Durant was in and out of Pine Knot between 1895 and 1900, so his influence seems plausible.

Pine Knot's progress from primitivism to rusticism, an expression closer to the urbane tastes of the Durants, is evident in photographs of the interiors. Other camps in the region followed the same rapid evolution. The earliest practice was to build with logs, their exteriors left intact and the inner face being hewn and the spaces between filled with plaster or cement (Fig. 40). The next step was to cover these striped walls once their novelty had faded. Curtains and carpets were used, but a more practical covering was resin-coated paper, much of which may be found at Pine Knot today. The paper, heavy and water-proof, covered most walls, as well as the undersides of the roofs which formed the ceilings of the early cabins.

A drawback to log construction was that the dimensions of a log cottage were limited, as a practical matter, to the trees that were available of a certain length, thickness and regularity. Frame construction allowed for greater flexibility. The Swiss Cottage at Pine Knot employed log construction on the first floor and frame construction on the second floor, possibly an indication of its transitional character. Moss was used as caulking between the logs, but the rough interior log facing was covered in the living room with vertical pine boards having beaded edges (Fig. 45). Similar wainscoting in the houseboat at Pine Knot was analyzed microscopically as yellow pine, indicating that Durant and others were importing some of their lumber from Virginia or the Carolinas for finished work in the Adirondacks, for the all-wood interiors that were popular in houses built after the Civil War.

The cottage for William and his wife introduced two features that would be repeated at William's later camps. These were stained pine planking, laid horizontally and deeply beveled at the edges, so as to resemble hewn logs; and the migration of birch bark from the overmantel or chimney breast to the ceiling (Fig. 48). Camp Uncas and Kamp Kill Kare made liberal use of beveled planking. The ceiling of the Recreation Hall was lavishly covered with birch bark sheets placed between exposed, peeled log rafters. Birch bark became an acceptable material for covering walls — particularly in the dining room — at large camps designed by architects in the Adirondacks in the next century. Unblemished bark was not easy or cheap to obtain, but besides its rustic character and durability it possessed the merit of brightening interiors that tended to be dim due to stained woodwork, shade trees and overcast Adirondack days.

The Durant stone fireplaces were individual creations. The hearth and fireplace in the Durant Cottage were smooth except for stippling on the stone face. The mantel and chimney breast, a safe distance above, were of birch bark and cedar (Fig. 48). The fireplace in the Recreation Hall was pyramidal and used an arched opening with a keystone; stones of

22

two colors, roughly hewn, were employed. William's emphasis on the stonework at his camps was illustrated by an incident in which he ordered a project dismantled because a stone had been put in backwards, i.e., the cut side faced out. Schuyler Kathan was one of Durant's chief masons and the man responsible for much of the outstanding stonework found in the Raquette Lake region. Kathan moved to Blue Mountain Lake in 1879, did some guiding, but principally worked as a stonemason, directing other masons by the time of his retirement about 1930.

Camp Pine Knot was a small village when William West Durant turned it over to Collis P. Huntington in 1895. Every building and each room was ready for occupancy. The inventory of furnishings lists hundreds of items, too many to recount here except for the "sitting room" which invites comparison with the photograph of the room in Figure 45:

1 Brown carpet	1 Pair andirons
1 Large rug	1 Iron fire fender
1 Small Rug	1 Set fire irons
1 Piano	1 Bellows
1 Sofa, 5 sofa pillows	1 Portiere [a curtain across a doorway]
1 Large arm chair	4 Red curtains
1 Rustic gun rack	4 Deer heads
1 Rustic standing lamp	1 Writing pad
2 Rustic tables	1 Wooden letter paper rack
1 Rustic book case	3 Stuffed birds
2 Rocking chairs	1 Rustic piano stool
1 Rustic armchair	2 Wrought iron lanterns
2 Chairs	1 Cuspidor
Electric bell	1 Round cushion
1 Japanese screen	1 Rustic clock
1 Wire fire screen	1 Cushion filled with balsam
2 Students lamps	1 Piano cover
1 Wood box (rustic)	

The glitter of a formal dinner in the dining room can be imagined from the glass, silver and china in the pantry, which was supplied with place settings for about twenty-four guests, as shown by the following for glassware alone:

24 Water glasses	1 Glass sugar bowl
24 Champagne glasses	3 Claret decanters
24 Sherry glasses	5 Sherry decanters
24 Claret glasses	1 Vinegar cruet
24 Whiskey glasses	1 Oil cruet
24 Liquor glasses	3 Sherry decanters
12 Vichey glasses	12 Egg glasses
6 Salt shakers	1 Wooden bread board
12 Salt cups	1 Cork screw
8 Glass dishes	1 Champagne cutter
7 Glass pitchers	

Eleven dozen more glasses were on order from Lewis & Conger. There were eighteen chairs in the dining room, an extension table with ten leaves, and, on the windows, five pairs of "Turkey red curtains."

Camp Pine Knot was the testing ground for William West Durant and the "school" of workmen whom he employed and who would work on construction projects elsewhere on Raquette Lake and nearby lakes. In 1893–94, when William started to build Camp Uncas, described in Chapter 9, he had about fifteen years of experience at Pine Knot behind him. The later projects, unlike Pine Knot, would follow master plans largely conceived by William himself. A consequence was that the random evolution of rustic effects at Pine Knot were subordinated to an overall decorative scheme at Uncas, in which, for example, entire suites of locally manufactured furniture — beds, chests of drawers, tables — were produced from a few standard designs and installed at Camp Uncas, Sagamore and later at Kamp Kill Kare. This was contrary to that *recherché* character that Seneca Ray Stoddard discerned at Pine Knot in 1888, by which he meant that the camp possessed qualities that were rare and precious. And so it was. The charm of log cabins, bark wrapped fireplaces and rustic furniture fashioned from twigs and limbs was wearing thin, and William felt that it was time to move on to a more suave and grand conception of the Adirondack camp, in which peeled pine ceiling beams and large stone fireplaces would not be all that removed from the secure recesses of the town houses and club rooms which he and his peers were familiar with in New York City.

Camps in the vicinity of Raquette Lake each usually had a few pieces of rustic furniture. Camp Pine Knot perhaps had more than most, at least 24 items by count in the 1895 inventory, nine in the living room of the Swiss Cottage and the rest in the main cottages. Of cedar and bark, rustic furniture was sparingly distributed, never making up more than a few pieces in a given room. Wicker furniture and factory-made furniture were more in evidence. Durant's later camps would not incorporate as much rustic furniture as Pine Knot did, the bark-covered variety in particular. It is likely that the ideosyncratic nature of rustic furniture (i.e., no two pieces were exactly alike), combined with its proclivity to peel and shed bark, spelled its end as a serious solution in the coming era of Adirondack camps designed by professional architects.

Employment in the Adirondacks was a catch-as-catch-can business, and the boom in camp and hotel construction after 1880 meant that the majority of men in the region had some knowledge of carpentry. Some were good only for rough carpentry ("wood butchers"), and others did finished work. Among the latter were a few who had a talent, acknowledged by their fellow workers, for piecing together railings, wall sidings and other trim from unbarked poles and sheets of bark. If there were few carpenters who were specialists at rustic work in cottage construction, still fewer were those who made rustic furniture. There were perhaps a dozen men in Raquette Lake in the first category, only four or so in the last. Of candidates for furniture manufacture, the most important was Joseph O. A. Bryere (Fig. 71), a Canadian by birth and an employee at Camp Fairview and Camp Stott in the 1880's. Several of Stoddard's guidebooks singled Bryere out as "an artist in rustic work," suggesting Bryere as the principal source of rustic furniture found at camps in the vicinity of Raquette Lake. Five of his pieces were given to the Adirondack Museum in 1975 by his daughter Clara Bryere. These had been built for the hotel which he and his wife opened on the lake about 1888, Brightside-On-Raquette.

We do not know who made the rustic furniture at Camp Pine Knot. Bryere is the most likely choice. Another possibility is Frank Farten, about whom nothing is known except the following entry in the May 24, 1900 issue of the *Warrensburg-Lake George News:* "Raquette Lake: Frank Farten has just finished one of the finest pieces of rustic work that has ever been put together in this country. The scene represents a hunter in the act of shooting. The picture is composed on birch bark, twigs and moss as they grew in natural colors. It is now at Pine Knot and is pronounced by skilled workmen to be the finest thing of its kind ever produced." Farten probably came from one of the outlying towns reached by the newspaper. He was a carpenter, for he had a hand in building Camp Omonsom, described below, for William West Durant and Dr. Arpad Gerster. He would seem to have possessed the skills to make rustic furniture.

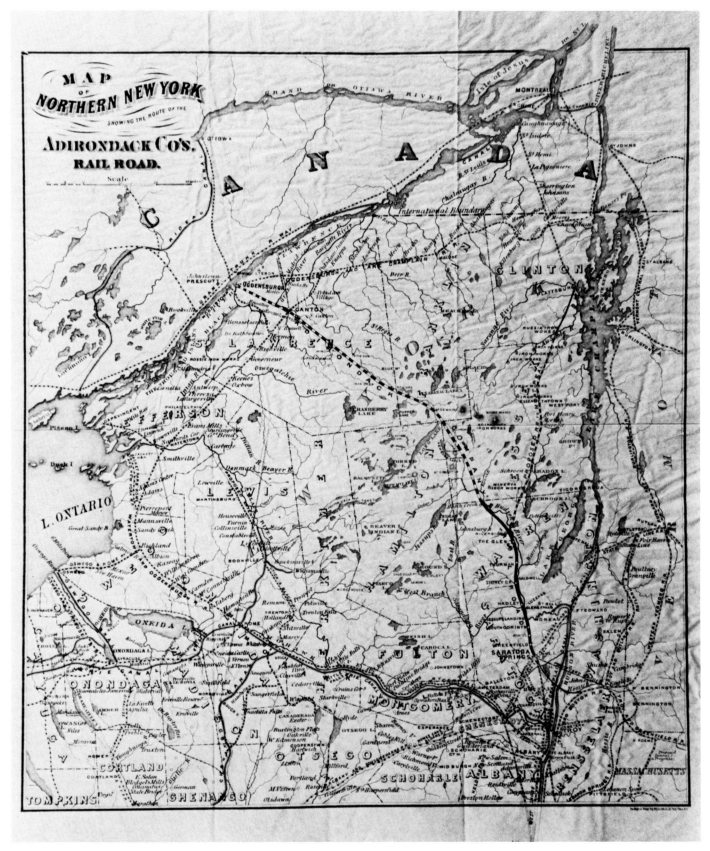

Fig. 5   *From the pamphlet "The Adirondack Company: Its Railroad and Estate," published in 1872, this map shows the completed portion of Dr. Durant's railroad from Saratoga Springs to North Creek, together with its proposed extension, never constructed, to Ogdensburg, N.Y., on the St. Lawrence River. Adirondack Museum.*

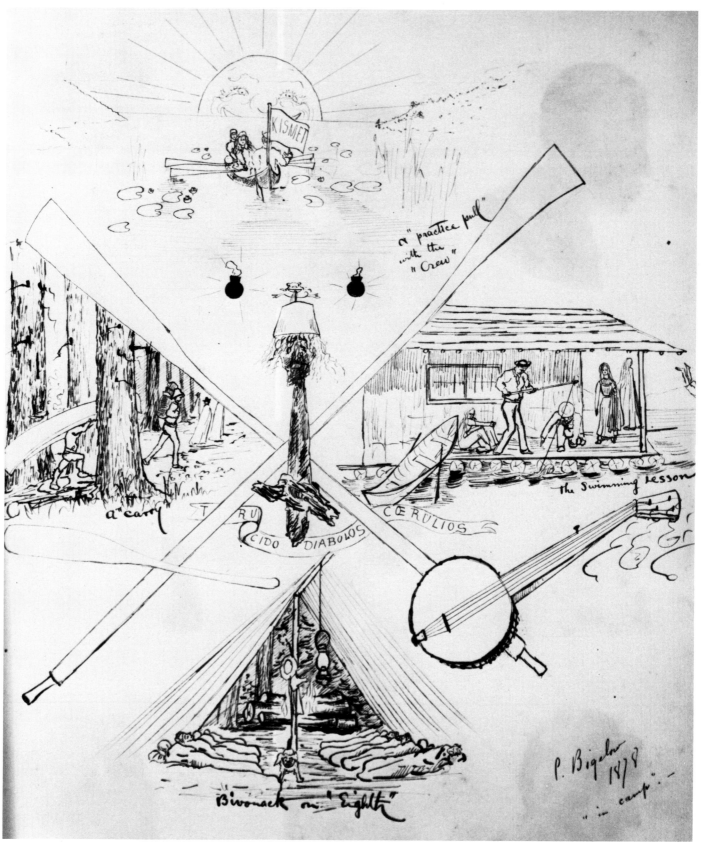

Fig. 6 Drawing in pen and ink from the guest book at Camp Pine Knot, page size 10-1/4" × 14-1/4", signed "P. Bigelow/1878." Activities "in camp" are shown, including swimming and fishing from a raft with cabin. Adirondack Museum.

Fig. 7   This photograph was taken about 1881 when Dr. Durant's residence in North Creek was extensively remodeled. Dr. Durant died here in October, 1885. The house burned about 1969. Adirondack Museum.

Fig. 8   William West Durant liked this portrait of himself, to judge by its appearance on a table at Sagamore Lodge in Fig. 84. It was taken in Saratoga Springs by Record & Epler, perhaps at the time of his marriage in 1884, when he was thirty-four. Adirondack Museum.

Fig. 9 William and Janet Stott Durant were newlyweds when this studio photograph was made in Saratoga Springs on February 24, 1885. Dr. Durant had survived an operation two years earlier but he would die at his North Creek home within eight months. Adirondack Museum.

Fig. 10   As a memorial to his father, William constructed this bridge in 1891 across the channel between Blue Mountain Lake and Eagle Lake. The bronze tablet to Dr. Durant may be seen underneath in a photograph by Seneca Ray Stoddard of about 1892. Called the "Pioneer Bridge," it is seen today by people in boats passing through the Eckford Chain of Lakes. Adirondack Museum.

Héloïse Durant

Fig. 11   Ella had been living in London for several years when her book Dante, A Dramatic Poem *was published in 1889. This photogravure portrait, showing her in her thirties, was the frontispiece. Adirondack
Museum.*

Fig. 12 *A photograph of about 1880 shows the office in lower Manhattan of the sugar refinery business owned by Dr. Durant's brother, Charles. Charles' three sons, Charles, Jr., Howard and Frederick (who stands in the doorway), each owned rustic camps in the Adirondacks. Adirondack Museum.*

Fig. 13 *Frederick Clark Durant leans against the post of the Prospect House verandah in a photograph taken in 1888 by E. H. Suplee. His wife, a member of the Harrison family of Philadelphia, is seated immediately in front of him. Adirondack Museum.*

Fig. 14　*The tools of the deer hunt, including dogs for driving, are displayed in a photograph by E. H. Suplee of 1888. Howard Durant reclines meditatively at the campsite on Moose Pond, located a few miles north of his summer home on Little Forked Lake. Adirondack Museum. Fig. 15 below. Alonzo Mix took this picture of the Lounsbury party setting off from Echo Camp on a fishing expedition in the company of three guides, about 1893. Phineas C. Lounsbury, governor of Connecticut in 1887–89, displays a gold chain on his ample midsection. The rifles were probably for a chance shot at a deer. Photograph courtesy of Francis Havinga.*

Fig. 16   Camp Stott had a half dozen school-girls who wore jerseys with the letter 'A" on the front after their rowing boat "Ariel." Admiral Edward T. Nichols is seated with Mrs. Frank Stott (her head averted) in this picture taken in 1885 by J. F. Holley. Adirondack Museum. Fig. 17, below. "A Musicale at Little Forked (Flash Light)" is the caption for this photograph of 1888 by E. H. Suplee. Mr. and Mrs. Howard Durant, the owners of the camp, are to the right. Adirondack Museum.

Fig. 18 Janet Stott Durant posed in an elegant dress of satin and lace on a visit to Paris, probably during a trip to Europe with her husband on his yacht in 1891 or 1892. Adirondack Museum.

Fig. 19 *William commissioned Neafie & Levy of Philadelphia to build him a yacht in 1890. Completed at a cost of about $200,000, the 191 foot ship attracted much admiration when it sailed into New York harbor on April 19, 1891. European royalty was entertained on the Utowana, as indicated by the inscription in William's hand on this photograph of 1892: "To His Imperial Highness/Prince Henry of Prussia." Adirondack Museum.*

Fig. 20 *Building a yacht was one thing, but sizable outlays were needed for maintenance and crew. The Utowana's stewards and cooks are shown in this picture of 1892. Adirondack Museum.*

Fig. 21 J. Beaver Webb designed William's yacht, as well as two others for J. Pierpont Morgan. The "dining saloon" of the Utowana, illustrated here, has the window seats and tidy organization found at Camp Uncas, sold by Durant to Morgan in 1896. Adirondack Museum.

Fig. 22 The New York Daily Tribune *of November 26, 1899 carried a picture of Ella and her son Timbrell with a story of the successful outcome of her suit against her brother. She carried her forty-six years lightly, to judge by this photostat picture from an abraded microfilm copy of the newspaper.*

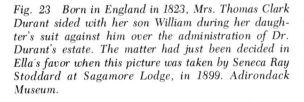

Fig. 23 *Born in England in 1823, Mrs. Thomas Clark Durant sided with her son William during her daughter's suit against him over the administration of Dr. Durant's estate. The matter had just been decided in Ella's favor when this picture was taken by Seneca Ray Stoddard at Sagamore Lodge, in 1899. Adirondack Museum.*

Fig. 24   Thwarted from business, he said, because of his sister's continuing law suits, William West Durant derived some income by conducting title searches on Adirondack lands. He was about 65 in this photograph, taken on Osprey Island and used as evidence in the Ladew suit. Adirondack Museum, gift of Charles E. Snyder.

Fig. 25 *In 1931, William stayed at Eagle's Nest, a visitor to projects which he had developed. Well dressed and erect, as always, he stands in front of the dining buildings at Camp Uncas, which he sold to J. Pierpont Morgan in 1896. Adirondack Museum.*

Fig. 26 *William was interred in the family's mausoleum, built in Brooklyn's fashionable Green Wood Cemetery in 1873 for $60,000. His sister Heloise was not to have a place there. Author's photograph.*

Fig. 27 *"Mission of the Good Shepherd," 1881, oil on canvas, by J. W. Ehninger. Dr. Durant and his son donated St. Hubert's Island and helped build a church and rectory on it for reasons that probably had less to do with piety than attracting prosperous families to Raquette Lake. The picture was painted a year after the church's consecration. Adirondack Museum.*

Fig. 28 *"Prospect House," before 1888, etching on card. This promotional card shows one of William West Durant's steamboats and the hotel built and operated by his cousin, Frederick Clark Durant. Opened in 1882, the hotel was far larger than any other on Blue Mountain Lake, accommodating up to 500 guests. Adirondack Museum.*

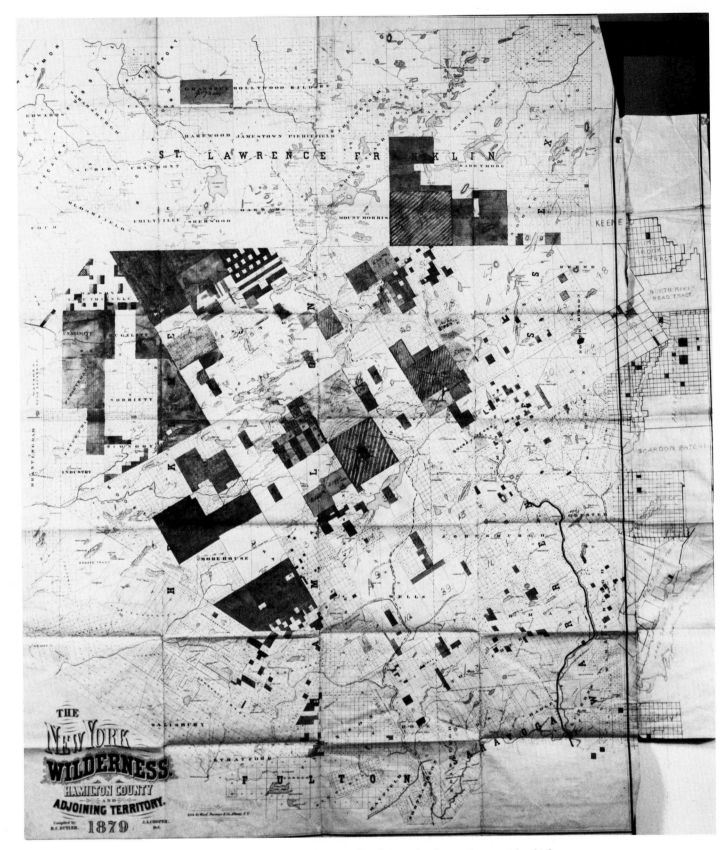

Fig. 29 This large map, "The New York Wilderness," indicates the thoroughness with which the Durants plotted their existing and potential holdings of lands in the Adirondacks. The shadings have not, however, been identified or dated. Adirondack Museum.

Fig. 30 This photograph of 1888 shows the railroad station in North Creek served by the Adirondack Railroad. The stage carried travellers over rough roads to Blue Mountain Lake, about 38 miles and 7-1/2 hours distant. Adirondack Museum.

Fig. 31 Collis P. Huntington befriended William West Durant, buying Camp Pine Knot and lending money to the younger man between 1895 and 1900, secured by mortgages against Durant's properties. The portrait was a gift to Durant. Adirondack Museum.

Fig. 32 In 1896, a crew of about forty men cut an 8-1/2 mile road through the forest to Eagle Bay, so Durant, Huntington and Morgan would find it easier to reach their camps from the railroad station at Clearwater. Durant, no armchair supervisor, assisted with the survey. Adirondack Museum.

Fig. 33 Huntington inspected the right of way for the Raquette Lake Railway with Durant, center, and the attorney, Charles E. Snyder, left. Completed in 1900, the 18 mile road made it possible to reach Raquette Lake directly from New York City overnight. Adirondack Museum.

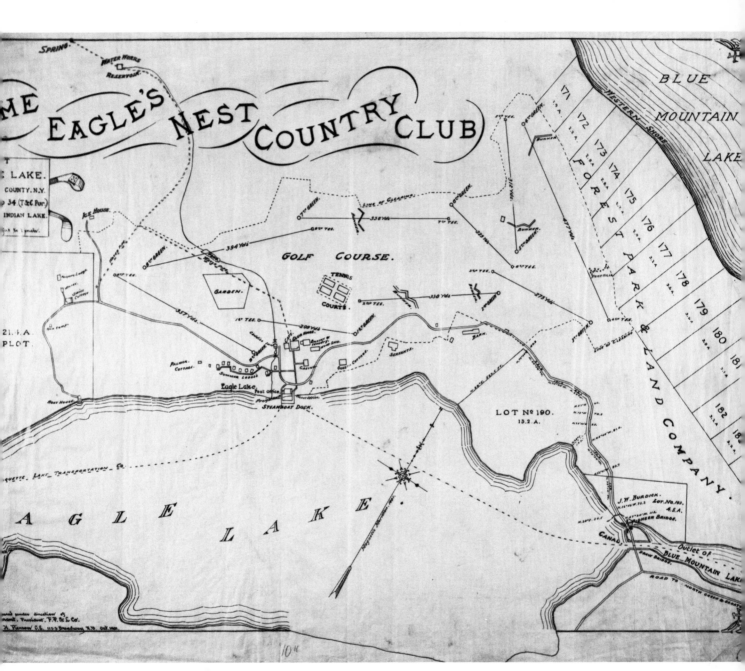

Fig. 34 In 1900, the Eagle's Nest Country Club opened with exhibition matches and dancing in the Casino. The map, dated October, 1901, shows the 21.4 acre plot reserved by William for himself, the "Pioneer Bridge" (Fig. 10) he built in memory of his father, and some of the lots he needed to sell to pay his growing debts. Adirondack Museum.

Fig. 35 A chalet completed for Durant at Eagle's Nest in September, 1900. The foreman, Josh Smith, in the derby hat, had worked on other Durant projects, including Sagamore Lodge. Adirondack Museum.

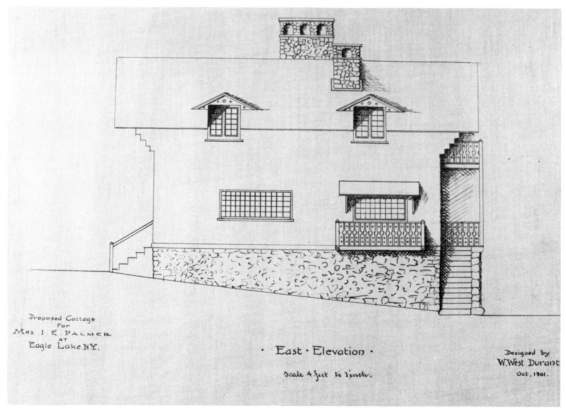

Proposed Cottage
For
Mrs I. E. Palmer
at
Eagle Lake, N.Y.

· East · Elevation ·

Scale 4 feet to 1 inch.

Designed by
W. West Durant
Oct, 1901.

Fig. 36 William West Durant's reliance on professional architects is unclear, but there is no question that he designed several cottages, as indicated by his plan for a Swiss chalet, never built, on Eagle Lake. Adirondack Museum.

Fig. 37-1, 2, 3   Using a locomotive and cars like those in cities, William opened the Marion River Carry Railroad in 1900, thereby linking his steamboats on Raquette Lake with those on the Eckford Chain of Lakes. The railroad, only three-quarters of a mile in length, operated until 1929. In 1955 the locomotive and one passenger car were given to the Adirondack Museum. Restored, they are seen by thousands of visitors who come to the museum in Blue Mountain Lake each summer. Rassie Scarrit is at the throttle in a photograph taken by E. Kellogg in 1911. See next page for Fig. 37-3.

Fig. 37-3   *Adirondack Museum, gift of Mr. and Mrs. Herbert A. Birrell.*

DEF. EX. D

Fig. 38 *Alvah Dunning, a colorful trapper and guide, occupied shanties at three locations. This one, covered with spruce bark, helped establish Joseph Ladew's claim to Osprey Island in ejection suits brought by the State after 1897. The photograph, taken about 1873, was submitted as evidence. Adirondack Museum.*

Camps
Cedars, Fairview, Echo

Camp Pine Knot borrowed a Swiss accent with its chalet, but Camps Cedars, Fairview and Echo, all of which were started and essentially completed between 1879 and 1885, each possessed a tripartite lodge whose facade bore a stamp of the classically inspired estate architecture developed in Britain during the eighteenth century — two towers flanking a gabled center. It is risky to compare these log structures with monuments like Holkham Hall (1734–59), with its 344 foot long facade, but the basic formal elements are there and should be mentioned, not so much to suggest an influence as to indicate the intention of the Durant family to introduce an architectural fillip to the vernacular building traditions of the region.

The lodges at Camps Cedars and Camp Fairview were built for Dr. Durant's nephews; a third, at Camp Echo, the only survivor, was erected for Phineas C. Lounsbury on land adjoining Pine Knot. Excluding porches, the three essentially consisted of a one-story cabin, about 20 feet wide and 30 feet deep, flanked by two-story attached towers that were each about 12 feet wide by 24 feet deep. Besides the striking appearance, a benefit of the twin tower plan must have been its compactness. Each tower contained two rooms, one over the other, and the cottage between them had one (Camp Fairview, Camp Echo) or two (Camp Cedars) rooms open to the rafters, making a total of five or six rooms enclosed by a minimal number of logs. The lodges differed in the treatment of their rustic porches and in a few details, such as windows, but they all were derived, to judge by their exteriors at least, from a single plan probably drawn by an architect. The arrangement of buildings varied at each camp, however, an expression perhaps due as much to differences between sites as to the preferences of the families.

Camp Cedars

Camp Cedars was the best integrated of the towered camps. It was started in 1880 on Forked Lake on a tract of thirty acres for Frederick Clark Durant (1853–1926). Frederick was the son of Dr. Durant's brother and a partner in his father's sugar refinery in New York (Fig. 12) until he turned to the construction and management of the Prospect House on Blue Mountain Lake, a large hotel (Fig. 28) whose history and lavish appointments are related in Harold K. Hochschild's book, *Township 34*. Frederick and his family summered at Camp Cedars and lived in Philadelphia, the home of his wife, Clara, a daughter of Joseph Harrison, Jr., a locomotive and bridge builder to the government in Czarist Russia.

Photographs of Camp Cedars reveal that the complex consisted of a series of attached buildings on a single axis. First was the three-part log lodge (Fig. 53) with its distinctive towers; behind was a covered porch, perhaps twelve feet long, which was connected to a log cottage (Fig. 58) that contained a kitchen, helps' dining room and laundry; the third building, sheathed with spruce bark, was a combination ice house, cooler and store house.

To the left of the lodge was the "Wigwam," a gathering place judging by a woodcut illustration of the interior in *Harper's Weekly* for November 17, 1883. Parallel with the lodge group, and only about thirty feet from it, were the nursery-buildings, shorter and lower but likewise consisting of two or three attached log cottages strung out in a file. Boardwalks and entrances enabled people to walk around and between the buildings, and to enter and leave a room without intruding on the privacy of another. The second floor rooms were reached by outside stairs at the rear of each tower (Fig. 54).

Edward Bierstadt, the brother of the painter, Albert Bierstadt, photographed a number of camps and scenic sites in the Adirondacks about 1885. Hired by Dr. Durant or his son, Bierstadt published his fine pictures in a one-volume work, *The Adirondacks, Artotype Views Among the Mountains and Lakes of the North Woods*, in an undated, autographed limited edition of forty-five copies. A two-volume edition, smaller in format but with more illustrations, appeared about 1886. Many of the pictures were of subjects related to the transportation, land and hotel interests of the Durant family, but the books were done tastefully, without a hint that the Adirondacks were being promoted.

Clues in Bierstadt's photographs allow us to reconstruct the interior of the main lodge at Camp Cedars. In front, facing Forked Lake, was a master room open to the rafters and dominated by a fireplace, overmantel and chimney wrapped in birch bark and framed by cedar poles (Fig. 56). A large four-post cedar bed stood in the corner next to the fireplace; a similar bed may partly be seen through the door of the adjoining room, the lower room of one of the towers. On the other side of the fireplace wall was the other room in the cottage, the dining room, which occupied about one-third of the lodge's floor area (Fig. 57). The fireplaces in the master room and dining room thus shared a common wall and chimney. A small room attached to the dining room — structurally a part of the breezeway — may have been a pantry.

Photographs predating Bierstadt's indicate the same evolution from primitive to finished rustic that was then occurring at Camp Pine Knot. The exposed hewn log and cement caulked walls and the resin papered overmantel of about 1880 (Fig. 55) were replaced by Bierstadt's time with smooth walls of unpainted boards and elaborate rustic trim for the fireplace and chimney.

The main cottage's chimney outside was of round stone construction, but a randomly coursed ashlar chimney like those at William West Durant's camps, quite different in quality and character, was built above a massive stone fireplace in the kitchen or laundry. An interesting and perhaps unique feature was the fireplace situated in the center of the Wigwam (Fig. 59), a free-standing cottage for family gatherings. It was formed of a hexagonally shaped hearth, built up about ten inches off the floor and partially filled with rocks, over which a metal funnel with stovepipe was placed to catch smoke and sparks. The funnel could be adjusted by pulleys to achieve the best draft.

The names of several area men have been associated with the construction of Camp Cedars. Harold K. Hochschild said that Alvah Dunning (c. 1814–1902) and Seth Pierce (c. 1829–c. 1915) helped to build the camp in 1880. An extraordinary corner cupboard from Camp Cedars was given to the Adirondack Museum by Frederick Clark Durant, Jr., who said it had been made by Pierce. The surface of the cupboard (Fig. 61) is decorated with geometric patterns fashioned from split twigs of eleven species and varieties of trees and shrubs. In 1906 Pierce testified, "My occupation is guiding, fishing, and hunting and once in a while I take my tools and go at carpenter work." He also did blacksmithing and had been a soldier in the Civil War.

A third candidate for some of the work at Camp Cedars, according to a couple of

Durant family members, was Andrew Fisher (d. 1918), who was employed as a carpenter, guide and as a caretaker at Camp Endion on Long Lake. Fisher probably made the mosaic twig sideboard at Endion about 1890. Kenneth Durant (1889–1972), a son of Frederick Clark Durant, said that he thought that Sunset Cottage at Camp Cedars had been built by Fisher.

The only building at Camp Cedars which survives is Sunset Cottage (Fig. 60), moved by sled across the ice of Little Forked Lake to its present location at Whitney Park shortly after 1936 when Camp Cedars was sold by Mrs. Frederick Clark Durant to Mrs. Harry Payne Whitney. Camp Cedars was being restored when World War II broke out. Many of its buildings were severely damaged by fallen hemlocks and pines during the Great Blowdown of November, 1950, and the camp was removed by Mr. C. V. Whitney. Named for the radiating rustic pattern in its gables (similar rustic work was done at Brandreth Park), Sunset Cottage is diminutive, twelve by fifteen feet, but it is a paradigm of rustic craftsmanship in the Adirondacks and a valuable reminder of Camp Cedar's all-but-vanished glory.

Besides the structures already mentioned, Cedars had others which were roughly outlined from memory by Kenneth Durant on a sheet of paper among his papers at the Adirondack Museum. Some of these features may have been introduced after 1900: open camp; two docks; summer house; water tower; store house and woodshed; guides' house and open camp; a winter house; dog kennel; power plant; workshop; chicken house; pig pen; barn; woodshed with saw; milking shed; sugar house; one or two spring houses. Bathrooms were located in the main and nursery complexes; in addition, there was a bath and water-closet behind the kitchen and two privies in the vicinity of the winter house.

Camp Fairview

Whereas the towered lodge at Cedars was the drum major behind which the other buildings followed in an orderly file, no such integrated pattern was evident at Camp Fairview, which was begun a year earlier, 1879, but progressed in fits and starts over the next six years. The location of Fairview on the western tip of Osprey Island presented a problem. Three of the four sides of the lodge faced the lake (Fig. 62), with the consequence that the builders attempted to offer three facades to the public instead of one, as at Cedars and Echo Camp. The two flights of stairs to the upper bedrooms in the towers were placed on each of the long sides of the lodge, which eliminated symmetry but achieved an ambiguity in which no side could be construed as a backside by passersby and neighbors, including the worshippers and resident rector at the Episcopal church on St. Hubert's Island hardly seven hundred feet distant.

Instead of two rooms, the central cottage at Fairview contained but one room, with the fireplace located in a side wall (Fig. 63) rather than in the partition wall as at Camp Cedars. Thus the cottage must have been shorter than its companion at Cedars by twelve or so feet.

Camp Fairview was built for Charles W. Durant, Jr. (1849–1928), the older brother of Frederick Clark Durant and a cousin of William West Durant, who handled Charles's affairs on Raquette Lake during this period, 1879–85. William assisted in getting Alvah Dunning to sell Osprey Island to Charles in 1879–80 and he made representations in Albany in an effort, related elsewhere, to have the state lease and then sell the 17 acre island and a 160 acre tract on the mainland to his cousin. Charles later said, in testimony given in 1917, that William had supervised the construction of Camp Fairview and that he thought that Darwin Parker had been the principal builder. Another statement in the legal record noted that "Charles W. Durant sent out and got Alvin Parker and gave him, Parker, the plans to build by." Darwin Parker had been a resident of Indian Lake since the 1850's and his son, Alvin, who was 29 years old in 1880, would seem to have worked with his father on the project.

Other men who are known to have worked at the camp were Charles Bennett and Joseph O. A. Bryere, both of whom built the second floor on the main lodge in 1883 and assisted in the construction of the boat house in 1883 or 1884. The Bryeres were employed as caretaker and cook at the camp, but in the late eighties took their services to Camp Stott, as indicated by an entry dated July 4, 1890 in a journal kept by the Stott family, "J.O.A. Bryere & family left camp — a Mr. Henry Brown of Indian Lake arrived to take charge." Alvah Dunning and Seth Pierce were said by Harold K. Hochschild to have worked on Camp Fairview, and Kenneth Durant believed that Andrew Fisher may have had a hand in it as well. The four men hired by Charles in 1879 to "locate" the camp on Osprey Island, and forced, in the words of one, to "skedaddle" when confronted by a weapon-wielding Alvah Dunning, were probably all carpenters of sorts: Seth Pierce, the brothers Edward and Richard Bennett (Charlie Bennet was a third brother), and George Pashley. The repetition of names here and at camps elsewhere is good circumstantial evidence identifying the members of the "Durant School" of rustic craftsmen working in the Raquette Lake region before the turn of the century.

When Charles sold his camp to a New York leather merchant, J. Harvey Ladew, in 1891, the complex consisted of the following structures: The towered cottage, an adjoining cottage containing a dining room, kitchen and servants' quarters, a large boathouse with accommodations for men servants above, an open camp, a barn, stable and hen house, an ice house and cooler, a stone breakwater, a steamboat dock,* a bridge to Little Osprey Island, a tennis court, and "other things," such as fences around the gardens. The adjoining island, an outcropping of rock with a few trees, was used as a playground for small children at the camp. The desirability of Osprey Island as a camp site, William testified, was that it was relatively free from flies and other insects that pestered occupants of camps and hotels on the mainland. A fire about 1920–30 destroyed the lodge and one or two other buildings at Camp Fairview.

Bierstadt illustrated only one interior at Camp Fairview, the room in the cottage between the towers. Like the early interiors at Pine Knot and Camp Cedars, the walls were of hewn and caulked logs. A second photograph (Fig. 64) shows that by 1906 the walls had been covered with the woodwork so widespread in nineteenth century homes: a chair rail with narrow beveled boards applied vertically above, and diagonal, more darkly stained boards below the rail. The fireplace was simply framed with cedar posts; its location on a low side wall rather than on an end wall formed by the gable eliminated the overmantel and chimney that, when wrapped in bark, provided a dominant focal point in the lodge at Camp Cedars. Fairview's principal windows — casement, each with sixteen square panes regularly set around a large rectangular pane — resembled some of those installed at Pine Knot at about the same time. The small window under the roof peak was a feature at most Durant camps, but here it was filled with small, irregularly shaped stained-glass panes, one of several decorative touches denoting prevailing stylistic accents brought into the region from afar, in this instance the Queen Anne Style and the Craftsman Movement. Also evi-

*Charles's steamboat *Stella* is displayed at the Adirondack Museum under another name, *Osprey*. Huntington used the boat on occasion.

dent is the prevailing passion at Adirondack camps of the eighties to adorn interiors with Japanese fans, parasols and prints, along with sundry other Victoriana, such as framed photographs of family members, shiny brass pots, dried flowers and the like, all of which may be seen to move but a few feet or inches, on mantel, shelf and table, during the course of a decade or so of dusting.

Artistic clutter was not to everyone's liking. On visiting Kamp Kill Kare, Dr. Arpad Gerster testily observed, "At the old camp we found Gov. Lounsbury sitting on the newly enlarged verandah, ornamented with artistic iron lamps and other city gimcracks. . . ." Two years earlier, on September 21, 1895, the distinguished Hungarian-born surgeon, who successively occupied two camps on Raquette Lake and another on Long Lake, wrote, "Some of our neighbors have introduced the American system of gadding about and never being without 'company.' From the first, we have declined to be drawn into this vortex of unrest and tedium." Dr. Gerster was not a recluse, for, as Harold Hochschild noted in *Township 34*, he entertained guests from New York City and treated the sick and injured during seasonal visits to the Adirondacks that spanned more than four decades.

Echo Camp

Echo Camp, the site of the third twin tower cottage, was started about 1883 at Long Point on Raquette Lake on a 10 to 12 acre tract squeezed between the Durants' Camp Pine Knot property and Charlie and Ed Bennett's hotel, "Under the Hemlocks." The camp was owned by Phineas C. Lounsbury (1844–1925), the governor of Connecticut in 1887–89 and president of the Merchants Exchange National Bank in New York City. Because of its size, the Lounsbury family, who resided in Ridgefield, Connecticut, required an extensive complex of cottages and service buildings for themselves and their servants and guides. In addition to the towered cottage (Fig. 65), the camp probably had the following by the turn of the century: several log cottages, the largest for Mr. and Mr. Lounsbury; a dining room and kitchen; guides' house; caretaker's house; laundry and wash houses; carpentry and paint shops; ice house; lean-to; dock; woodshed; a tea house; several wells and other structures, including privies. The caretaker occupied the only winterized building.

The two towers originally measured about 11 feet wide by 23 feet deep each and the cottage between, enclosing an all-purpose living room, was about 19 feet wide by 27 feet deep. Before 1897 a log extension, about 12 feet deep, was added across the back. This must have given the cottage a plan roughly like the twin tower cottage at Camp Cedars. If the original building at Echo had been too small, the living room in the center was apparently deemed to be too dark. The solution was a clearstory, with roof and glass sides, built over the roof peak nearly all the way from front to back. This novel addition, of about 1897, flooded the living room with light during the cloudiest Adirondack days.

The nearby cottage used by Mr. and Mrs. Lounsbury had bedrooms on one side and at the rear of the living room. The problem of providing access to a back room was solved by placing the stone fireplace to one side of the back wall, in the corner rather than in the center of the wall, as was the practice in most other camp cottages. A splendid picture window next to the entrance was surrounded by lead mullions into which were placed rectangles of amber, pink and blue glass around centers of colored "bulls-eye" glass globules (Fig. 66). The view from within of trees, lake and Big Island was thus softly framed by transparent colored glass.

54

The Lounsburys were a large and active group, to judge by photographs, one of which showed a party of men, women and children outfitted with fishing rods, rifles and two guideboats about to set forth on an Adirondack expedition in the company of four guides (Fig. 15). In September, 1901, the former governor of Connecticut wrote J. George Thompson from Echo Camp complaining about the new policy which prohibited private boats from using the dock belonging to the Raquette Lake Transportation Company on the Marion River Carry. Thompson, who was William West Durant's superintendent for the steamboat line, had followed orders handed down by the line's new co-owners. The policy, Lounsbury said, departed from eighteen years of patronage by his family on Raquette Lake, "severe treatment after so many years."

Echo Camp was used by a niece until about 1940, after which it was unoccupied until 1946 when it was purchased as a camp for girls, in which capacity it has served to the present day. The original buildings have withstood passing years and heavy summer use remarkably well. Mrs. Francis Havinga, the owner, built a long extension on the front of the twin tower camp. This considerably altered the appearance of the cottage, which otherwise remained intact.

Berkeley Lodge

A fourth twin tower cottage should be mentioned here. Built in 1896 on Second Lake for ex-President Benjamin Harrison, who named it Berkeley Lodge after his family's homestead in Virginia, it is of importance here because it was designed by the Herkimer architect, Charles E. Cronk. In 1899 Cronk wrote William West Durant about possible projects, to which William replied, on June 15, "At present I have nothing that I could give you to do for me, but of course later I may do more building, and may require the services of any [sic.] architect . . ." William did not imply that the architect had done any previous work for him, but Cronk's name cannot be dismissed out of hand as the source of the architectural plan for Camp Fairview which Charles W. Durant turned over to Alvin Parker about 1880.

Harrison was president when he visited the Adirondacks in 1892, the year of his defeat by Grover Cleveland. The next year a letter on his behalf was written by John B. Henderson, a U.S. Senator from Missouri in 1862–69 and owner of a camp on Raquette Lake, asking William for permission for Harrison and him to fish and hunt at Shedd (now Sagamore) Lake. According to Harold K. Hochschild, Henderson said that President Harrison was interested in acquiring a campsite on Raquette Lake from Durant.

Instead, Benjamin Harrison chose a site on Second Lake about twenty-five miles to the west, not far from Old Forge. His lodge (Fig. 67), still in good repair, was larger and more sophisticated than the twin tower cottages on Raquette Lake and Forked Lake. The towers and their roofs were octagonal instead of rectangular in section, and the living room in the center was two rather than 1½ stories high. The roof and the living room beneath were oriented from side to side rather than front to back. This provided greater space and also offered access from within the building to the bedrooms on the second floor of the towers, reached by stairs and landings at each end of the living room (Fig. 68). The lower two-thirds of Berkeley Lodge was sheathed with spruce logs, but the portions above the level of the eaves were shingled. An attached cottage at Berkeley Lodge contained the kitchen, dining room and Harrison's office. In addition, the camp had a house for guides and a boat house.

The combination of log and shingle, adopted in the 1880's in the Adirondacks [e.g., Little Forked Camp], may have been construed by architects and their patrons as a happy compromise between primitive and urban extremes of expression. Stanford White, perhaps New York's foremost architect, designed two large Adirondack residences, one for the Tytus family on Honnedaga Lake, about 1895, at which shingles above half-logs were employed as an exterior siding.

Little Forked Camp and Camp Stott

5

Little Forked Camp

When Howard Marion Durant (1859–1921) built his camp on a slope overlooking Little Forked Lake, he used an architectural design that was at once more spacious and less picturesque than the cottages erected by his brothers at Cedars and Fairview and his cousin William at Pine Knot. A photograph in Edward Bierstadt's limited edition version of *The Adirondacks* showed a full two-story cottage with a square hipped roof. Attached by a short covered breezeway at a rear corner of this cottage, identified in a photograph of 1892 as the "Wigwam," was a smaller building which may have enclosed the kitchen and dining room on the ground floor and a room or two for servants on the floor above (Fig. 73). These buildings were erected before 1885, the approximate date of Bierstadt's photographic tour of the Adirondacks. By 1892 a second full cottage, called "Deerland," had been built about sixty feet distant from the first.

Howard's cottages are of interest because they combined split-logs, shingles and clapboards on what otherwise would seem to be surburban residences. A deep porch with spruce posts and railings extended around three sides of the Wigwam, which was approached from below by two flights of stairs that met at a landing at the center of the porch. Exterior walls at this level were of spruce logs, probably half-logs over a planked frame. The upper floor was shingled and considerably larger, extending over the lower rooms and porch. Deerland cottage employed an L-shaped plan and was similar in general appearance to the Wigwam, except for the decorative courses of wedge-shaped shingles that alternated with plain shingles on the upper floor, and clapboarding applied to a portion of the cottage at the rear.

In the decades to come, roomy cottages of this type would appear in numbers in the Adirondacks. They were hybrids of the forest and suburb, with the suburban influence more clearly evident. And little wonder, since plans for such summer residences were often prepared by an architect in the city who would never visit the construction site. The rustic elements — logs, posts and poles — were tacked on, probably on the initiative of the contractor or project foreman, and at the behest of the architect. Substitution of finished for rustic materials would produce a house indistinguishable on the outside from a suburban residence in a middle class neighborhood.

Little Forked Camp's cottages were probably finished from the time of occupancy; that is, they did not require additional work as did the other Durant camps, but had interiors with walls, floors and even ceilings covered with milled boards. The living room or "Hall," as it was referred to in an album of photographs taken by H. H. Suplee in 1888, had a feature not found at Durant camps elsewhere. The stairs to the upper floor ascended over the fireplace, the top of which supported a landing between two short flights of steps (Fig. 74). Novel solutions to the problem of providing access to the upper rooms of summer homes, either to conserve space or to exploit the open space of living rooms extending from floor to roof rafters, became a challenge for architects at about this time. The arrangement

57

at Little Forked Camp must have been an early example of this experimentation in the Queen Anne Style.

Little is known about Howard Durant, but he evidently enjoyed outdoor sports and the company of family and friends. One photograph shows him outdoors (Fig. 14), while another depicts four women and three men entertaining one another in "A Musicale at Little Forked," with Howard holding a tambourine, two ladies with banjos and a third with a zither on her lap (Fig. 17). Howard was younger than his brothers Charles and Frederick, yet he succeeded in getting elected to membership in the New York Yacht Club in 1881 when he was scarcely twenty-two years old, ten years before William West Durant's election to the club in 1891. (Charles, Jr. also belonged, as did Dr. Durant, who had joined in 1865.) Harold K. Hochschild's *Township 34* relates that Howard loaned $28,000 to Frederick in 1888 to meet deficits of the Prospect House, and that he was "virtually in control" of the hotel by 1892. Howard was manager of the hotel in 1897–1900, having foreclosed on the first mortgage on January 11, 1898. Whether the loss was one of necessity, convenience or imposition of will by one Durant over another cannot be known, though instances of all three could be recited among the siblings of Dr. Durant and his brother Charles.

Camp Stott

The family of Frank H. Stott, co-owner of four woolen mills in Stottville, N.Y., made their first visit to Raquette Lake on August 17, 1876, at about the time of William West Durant's arrival that summer with his father and sister. For about thirty years thereafter, until 1905 or a little later, the Stott family and its guests returned to Raquette Lake where they joined in the life of the lake, enjoying to the hilt the lake's social and its private pleasures. The leatherbound Camp Stott journal, in the library at the Adirondack Musem, contained William's signature and the inscription, "My first call!!!," in 1880 [see Appendix].

Located on Bluff Point, on 160 acres of land which Mr. Stott leased from the state, the camp grew, like Camp Pine Knot, from a few cottages to a complex of more permanent structures that numbered about ten by 1886. Eventually the state permitted the Stotts to purchase the land, or perhaps the "improved" portion of it, for the property was sold to the magazine publisher, Robert J. Collier, in 1910 for $20,000.

The buildings at Camp Stott differed from those at the other camps associated with the Durant family. Cement caulking filled the interstices between the logs of the first cottage, built in 1878, which conveyed a pioneer appearance except for herringbone patterns worked out with split poles in the space formed by the gable at each end (Fig. 69). Instead of the entrance being placed at a gable end, as at Pine Knot, it was located on a side wall under the eaves. Two other cottages employed peeled logs, but these were deeply jointed at the corners for a tighter fit requiring only moss or oakum for caulking. All three cottages used a simple type of joint to lock the logs together — a flat or square notch joint. This contrasted with the saddle notch construction of early cottages at Pine Knot, in which the circular ends of the logs projected several inches beyond the walls at each corner.

Another early building at Camp Stott was a dining room with open sides and a kitchen attached at one end. A photograph of 1885 showed that striped canvas curtains were unrolled on the sides when it was wet or cold (Fig. 69). In 1884 an elderly visitor with muttonchop whiskers, Admiral Edward T. Nichols, wrote an affectionate letter of thanks to the five teenage girls whom he had taught to row as a crew during his visit (Fig. 16). Writing from the Prospect House in Blue Mountain Lake, he said, "I was hungry when I arrived, and soon found the dining room, a barn-like looking place with its three rows of small tables. What a contrast to Camp Stott with its open air dining room, its long, sociable table, its canvas walls, its breeziness, its good grub, but above all its [hearty?], whole souled kindness and good feeling, and its jollity." He added that ". . . in the few hours I've been here, I've seen more store clothes and store manners than I've seen for a fortnight."

Men and boys stayed at Camp Stott, but the journal suggests that the place was managed by Mrs. Stott and dominated by women. The girls, who wore sweathers emblazoned with the letter "A," for their boat, the "Ariel," named after the prankish character in Shakespeare's *The Tempest*, occupied the Spinsterage, in which four or five beds were tightly arrayed along one wall. Young people contributed much to the camp's gaiety and bustle, at least during the eighties. Mrs. Stott, who kept an eye on their comings and goings, usually arrived at the camp in May for a week or so of cleaning and fishing, the latter an activity which the women pursued, if anything, with as much skill as the male members of the family. Another spring chore was the cleaning of the Episcopal church and rectory on St. Hubert's Island. Except for spring visits, the camp was not occupied before July 15. Seldom did summer residents depart until September 1st at the earliest, sometimes remaining as late as the first week in October.

Mr. Stott arrived in August, perhaps in time for the "entertainment" which was held at the camp each summer to raise money for the Episcopal church. In addition to the caretaker and his wife, several others were seasonally employed as guides for the family and its guests. In 1887 these included Joseph O. A. Bryere (who, with his wife, was also caretaker in 1889–90), Willard Locke, Frank Emerson and Dennis Mahan. Three or four other guides were hired in late August and September of that year for driving deer with hounds: Jerome Wood, John Ballard, Ike Kenwell and perhaps Sidney Porter. Deer hunting, both with and without hounds, and at night from a boat with a lantern affixed to the bow ("jacking"), was an activity largely left to the men. The journal records only one winter visit, and that was at Camp Pine Knot for a two week period over Christmas and New Years, 1892–93, when the Durants and other members of the family held a dinner and dance for guides, residents and their families at the lake. About sixty attended the party and a newspaper story reported that each of the guests received a gift.

On July 31, 1886 Frank Stott decided that the Spinsterage and another log building should be removed and a new "rustic log house" erected on the site of the latter, probably the cottage with rustic work on its gable ends. The work was done by Thomas Wallace who lived in the Spinsterage with his family while the Stotts stayed at Camp Pine Knot nearby. Within a month the old building was down and the foundation for its replacement was ready and the floor timbers were being laid. On May 10 of the next year the journal recorded, "Arrived at Camp Stott about six p.m., taking possession of the new house and eating supper there."

The new house was unprepossessing on the outside. Probably of frame construction with half-logs applied to planking, it was two stories high with a simple gable roof that extended over a porch on two or three sides, according to an unclear photograph of 1888. Noteworthy, however, was the living room, really a two-story hall, with a flat ceiling of varnished boards and walls of the same material, but with an overlay of decorative woodwork bands that ran around the four sides of the room (Fig. 72). Nothing as spacious had been built at a private camp on Raquette Lake up to that time. The fireplace was entirely of brick, and carved under the mantel were the dates "1878" and "1886," the period of the first cottage on the site, and the Latin inscription MOLLIA TEMPORA, meaning "Happy Times." A Stoddard photograph of about 1890 shows the usual mix of summer furnishings — a large center table covered with a cloth, caned rocking chairs that would more likely be placed on porches outside the Adirondacks, a kerosene lamp on a rustic stand by an upright piano, mounted birds and deer heads on the walls, a carpet on the floor, and so on. The windows, rectangular with small panes, are the only structural feature which the room shared with other Durant camps. In its size, woodwork and stolid informality, the room was a departure from the cottage it replaced, a tangible symbol of gentility newly arriving in the wilds.

Nothing is known about the builder, Thomas Wallace. Bryere and a man named Town, perhaps of the Long Lake family, worked at Camp Stott, but the many guides and caretakers, such as George Jenkins, who were employed there, were candidates for the various projects at the camp calling for carpentry skills. The camp was enlarged to 20 buildings by Collier, but despite alterations by him and subsequent owners, the living room of the "new house" remains very much as it was more than a century ago.

The divorce of Janet and William West Durant must have been a painful event for the Stott family, though the journal gave no hint of any of the changed relationships and old summer rituals that must have occurred after 1896 as a consequence. By that time Pine Knot had been purchased by Collis P. Huntington, whose name is not mentioned in the journal, and the carefree girls and boys of the 1880's had become responsible adults in the nineties. In 1896 the family returned to their home in Stottville, named Brightside, by way of the railroad from Clearwater to Utica. This western route was more convenient, since it eliminated the long carriage ride to the railroad in North Creek. Familiar sights, such as Dr. Durant's former residence in North Creek, were also certain not to be encountered.

Camp life imparted a heightened sensitivity to the passage of time. Each summer began with the joy of reunion and closed with the pang of separation, and this cycle was seen to be a part of the rhythm of life itself. Birth, childhood, maturity and age were evident in the generations who populated the camp, but also in the camp itself and in the other local objects associated with summer life. A sense of loss was felt by the principal author of the journal, probably Mrs. Frank Stott, at a church service on St. Hubert's Island in August of 1899: "Mrs. Bonchee was the only person I knew. Old times came crowding back in my thoughts. It was almost too sad." An era in the life of the Stott family was soon to draw to an end, as Mrs. Stott seems to have known. The last dated entry in the journal, September 19, 1900, recorded twenty-four years after the first, and squeezed in the last remaining space at the bottom of the last available page, said, "All left for home. . . . Party separated at Albany. A glorious [day?], which ends this book."

Camp Pine Knot

Fig. 39 *This casual scene at Camp Pine Knot was staged to show that the Raquette Lake region was open for development. William leans against the window while his grey bearded father, Dr. Durant, is seated nearby. Photograph by Seneca Ray Stoddard, c. 1877. Adirondack Museum.*

Fig. 40   *The interior of one of the first cottages at Pine Knot, built about 1876 and still standing. Photograph by Stoddard, undated. Adirondack Museum.*

Fig. 41   *The "Summer Kitchen" of Pine Knot's first years was an improvised shelter. Photograph by Stoddard, c. 1877. Adirondack Museum.*

Fig. 42   *This open dining room at Pine Knot was later enclosed and a kitchen and dining building attached at the right. It stands today, though it has undergone alterations over the years. Photograph by Stoddard, before c. 1882. Adirondack Museum.*

Fig. 43   *William built a floating camp, called the "Barque of Pine Knot," which could be towed by a steamboat and anchored anywhere on Raquette Lake. Containing two bedrooms, a kitchen and two small baths, it is beached at Pine Knot today. Photograph possibly by Stoddard, undated. Adirondack Museum.*

Fig. 44   *The one story cottage in Fig. 39 was replaced about 1882 by this two story chalet. The photograph was taken c. 1885 by Edward Bierstadt, brother of the painter, Albert Bierstadt. The chalet still stands. Adirondack Museum.*

Fig. 45   *The "Sitting Room" of the chalet in the preceding illustration, photographed by Stoddard about 1893. Some of the furnishings at Pine Knot, such as the rustic bookcase, are found at Camp Pine Knot today. Adirondack Museum.*

Fig. 46   By 1888, Camp Pine Knot had discarded the rough edges of its early years and become a refined village of rustic cottages and service buildings within a grove of birch and evergreen trees, shown here in a Stoddard photograph. Adirondack Museum.

Fig. 47   *Slender and taller than average, William West Durant was photographed descending the stairs of the Durant Cottage, built about 1889 at Pine Knot for his wife and him. Note the bark covered walls, bay window and hewn stone chimney. The cottage is extant. Stoddard photograph, c. 1889. Adirondack Museum.*

Fig. 48   A recent photograph of the principal room in the Durant Cottage reveals the durability of bark and limbs as building materials. The bark ceiling, beveled wall boards and the textured, carefully proportioned stonework reflect Pine Knot's emergent rustic style under William's guidance. Photograph by Richard Linke (1974). Adirondack Museum.

Fig. 49   Bedstead formerly at Camp Pine Knot, cedar and birch bark, c. 1885–1895. Given to the Adirondack Museum by the Raquette Lake Girls and Boys Camp, this bedstead may have been made by Joseph O. A. Bryere (Fig. 71). Author's photograph.

Fig. 50 William built this "annex" about 1889–91 to provide additional space to the log cottage used by his mother, and nursery rooms for his three infant children and their nurse. Janet Durant holds her son, Basil, while the nurse watches. The complex still stands at Pine Knot. Photograph probably by Stoddard, c. 1891. Adirondack Museum.

Fig. 51 *The rustic portico of the Recreation Building at Camp Pine Knot. This large structure may have been built between 1895–1900, after the property had been sold to Huntington. Durant did not mention it in his 1895 inventory (see appendix). Author's photograph.*

Fig. 52 *Hearts, crosses and lyres fashioned from twigs and laid on birch bark on the bay window of the Recreation Building at Pine Knot (Fig. 51) constituted an intriguing experiment in exterior rustic decoration. Unfortunately it was not tried elsewhere. Author's photograph.*

Camp Cedars

Fig. 53 *This photograph by Edward Bierstadt shows the twin towered cottage and, to the left, the Wigwam at Camp Cedars as they appeared about 1885. Cedars was started in 1880 for the family of Frederick Clark Durant, the builder of the Prospect House (Fig. 28). Adirondack Museum.*

Fig. 54 The main lodge at Camp Cedars contained bedrooms in the towers, a combination bedroom and sitting room in the front of the central cottage, with the dining room at the rear. The stovepipe in this photograph of c. 1884 by Stoddard was later replaced by a stone chimney. Adirondack Museum.

Fig. 55 The combination bedroom-sitting room of the lodge at Camp Cedars, with a view of an adjoining bedroom, photographed by Stoddard before 1885. The hewn logs were later covered with boards, as illustrated below. Adirondack Museum.

Fig. 56 *The room in Fig. 55 when photographed c. 1885 by Edward Bierstadt. Notice the four-post cedar bed, mosaic twig pedestal table and bark-wrapped overmantel and fireplace. The national mania for Japan, evident here in the lanterns, fans and parasols, was widespread at Adirondack camps at this time. Adirondack Museum.*

Fig. 57 *The dining room at Camp Cedars, photographed by Edward Bierstadt c. 1885. The stairs outside the window locate the dining room in Fig. 54. Adirondack Museum.*

Fig. 58   *Behind the twin towered lodge at Camp Cedars were a succession of buildings containing staff dining room, kitchen, laundry, and the ice house and cooler. This sensitive photograph was taken on July 4, 1933 by Margaret Bourke-White, a friend of Kenneth Durant. Adirondack Museum, gift of Margaret Bourke-White.*

Fig. 59   *The Wigwam at Camp Cedars functioned as a gathering place for family and guests on evenings and rainy days. The fireplace with its adjustable stovepipe, shown in a Bierstadt photograph of about 1885, may have been unique to the central Adirondacks. Adirondack Museum.*

Fig. 60 *All the buildings at Camp Cedars, except for this one, Sunset Cottage, were demolished following extensive damage to the complex in the Great Blowdown hurricane of November, 1950. The cottage, only twelve by fifteen feet, but a superlative example of rustic construction, had been moved about 1936 to its present location on Little Forked Lake. Author's photograph, courtesy of Mr. and Mrs. C. V. Whitney.*

Fig. 61 *The corner cupboard at Camp Cedars utilized twigs from eleven varieties and species of trees and shrubs. It has been attributed to Seth Pierce, known for his rustic carpentry prior to 1900. Author's photograph. Adirondack Museum, gift of Frederick Clark Durant, Jr.*

Camp Fairview

Fig. 62 Camp Fairview, one of three camps in the Raquette Lake area with twin tower lodges, was built 1879–1885 for Charles W. Durant, Jr., near the site of the shanty shown in Fig. 38. New York State unsuccessfully tried to eject the family that bought Osprey Island and its camp in 1891. Photograph by Stoddard, 1888. Adirondack Museum.

Fig. 63 *The central cottage between the towers of the lodge at Camp Fairview had a fireplace in a side wall, a departure from the companion lodge at Camp Cedars (Fig. 56). The factory-made windows reflect fashionable decorative styles of the period. Photograph by Bierstadt, c. 1885. Adirondack Museum.*

Fig. 64 *Adirondack camps acquired a familiar clutter with the passage of years. The tidy room in the preceding illustration shows the same plaster figurine on the mantel in a photograph taken in 1906, nearly 21 years later. Adirondack Museum.*

Camp Echo

Fig. 65 The main lodge at Echo Camp, built c. 1883 and the only survivor of the towered camps in the region. This photograph of c. 1897, taken by A. L. Mix, shows part of the clearstory added by Gov. Lounsbury (Fig. 15) over the roof peak of the central cottage. Photograph courtesy of Francis Havinga.

Fig. 66 The cottage occupied by Gov. and Mrs. Lounsbury at Echo Camp had a picture window framed by amber, pink and blue tinted glass set in lead mullions. Photograph by Richard Linke (1974), Adirondack Museum.

Berkeley Lodge

Fig. 67 A later, more sophisticated version of the twin towered lodge was built in 1896 on Second Lake for Benjamin Harrison, U.S. President in 1889–93. Designed by Charles E. Cronk, of Herkimer, it was pictured in an article of c. 1901.

Fig. 68 President Harrison's Berkeley Lodge, named after his ancestral home in Virginia, was planned to give access to upstairs bedrooms from within. The camp is extant. This photograph is from an article of c. 1901.*

Camp Stott

Fig. 69 The "old building" at Camp Stott on Raquette Lake, built in 1878 and replaced in 1886 by the cottage containing the living room in Fig. 72. Nearby is an open dining room and the kitchen. The curtains were dropped in rainy or cold weather. The photograph was taken in August, 1885, by J. F. Holley. Adirondack Museum.

Fig. 70 *The grounds at Camp Stott showing two log cottages, evidence of a garden and newly planted trees, c. 1890. The path led to the dock. Adirondack Museum.*

Fig. 71 *Employees and others at Camp Stott are posed in front of the rustic laundry building in this photograph of c. 1890. On the porch are Mr. and Mrs. Joseph O. A. Bryere. He was known locally for his rustic furniture. Henry "Commodore" Bradley, far right, ran Durant's transportation system and later superintended his land transactions. Adirondack Museum.*

Fig. 72   *The living room of the "New House" at Camp Stott, in a Stoddard photograph of about 1888, departed from the primitivism of earlier camps. Carved under the mantel is "1878 MOLLIA TEMPORA 1886" (good times). This room is little changed today, though the property has undergone alterations in ensuing years. Adirondack Museum.*

Little Forked Camp

Fig. 73 *Howard M. Durant and his daughter, Maria, stand on the porch of the Wigwam in a photograph of 1892. No longer standing, the camp consisted of several two story cottages built c. 1885 on Little Forked Lake. The dining room, kitchen and staff quarters may have been in the adjoining building here. Adirondack Museum.*

Fig. 74 *"Hall at Little Forked Camp," photographed in 1888 by E. H. Suplee. The placement of the fireplace under the landing of stairs to rooms above was an architectural device that may have been new to the region. Adirondack Museum.*

Family Matters 6

Hostility and resentment kept the Durant household on edge during the years between the family's return from Europe and Dr. Durant's death in October, 1885. Years later, Heloise testified that her brother and father disagreed on many matters in that period, mostly over the unwillingness of Dr. Durant to give William a larger salary and greater responsibility in the family's business. William replied in kind, saying that his sister had been at odds with the entire family, not just their father but with their mother, as well. Mrs. Durant, for her part, complained that she got too little spending money from her husband.

Dr. Durant's true financial condition was known only to him. He said that he had little money to give, but this was due to his having created a perpetual indebtedness to his wife, settling a preference on her over others who might try to establish a claim on his own assets. However, he controlled the securities assigned to her, having long since been legally designated her "agent" in disposing of or adding to them. Almost all of the stocks and bonds of the Adirondack Company, embracing the railroad between Saratoga Springs and North Creek and many thousands of acres in the Adirondacks, were nominally placed in Mrs. Durant's name.

While Dr. Durant was building the Union Pacific Railroad in the 1860's, his wife and two children wandered from place to place in Europe. The house in North Creek, called "The Gables," replaced the family home in fashionable Brooklyn. Dr. Durant spent a good deal of time at his office in New York City and his wife and daughter often were off visiting relatives and friends in Albany and in New York and environs. William lived in Saratoga Springs where an office of the Adirondack Company was located. After his father's death he occupied a succession of camps in the Adirondacks and rented rooms at several luxurious residential hotels in New York City. Following her husband's death, Mrs. Durant and her companion, Miss Molineaux (a cousin, perhaps), made lengthy visits to Florida, Louisiana and California. They lived in Santa Barbara and Pasadena in 1894–96, and later resided in Lakewood, N.J. and Utica, N.Y. Complaints of poor health recur with revealing frequency in letters exchanged among family members from these far-flung places. Clearly, affection and understanding were stretched until Victorian propriety was the chief bond holding the family together.

Several complaints were lodged against Ella by the family in 1881. She was accused of keeping late hours (she was then 28), and disobeying her father's orders that Pine Knot not be opened that summer. More ominously, she was interested in a career on the stage, had written a life of Dante and was composing the poems that were to be published in 1884 in the collection, *Pine Needles Or Sonnets and Songs.* Her restlessness aroused anxiety in Dr. Durant's conventional household.

In July, Ella left the North Creek home without informing her father. Her mother, she said, had departed for a summer round of visits, and she took this as a signal for embarking on errands of her own, the first of which took her to an Episcopal convent in Peekskill, N.Y., where she remained until her confirmation four to six weeks later. She had wanted to enter the convent earlier, but the family, whom she described as "not church people," were unanimously opposed to it. She left the convent and stayed at the Northampton home of Mrs. John A. Dix, the wife of Governor Dix's nephew and a friend of the Durant family.

Dr. Durant had ample time that summer to nurse his anger. Ella, knowing a confrontation was in the offing, spoke to Mrs. Dix and others about her difficulties. The solicitous letters received by the doctor on her behalf merely added to his ire. He met her as she emerged from a jewelry store at Sixth Avenue and Twenty-Third Street and threatened to cast her out from his house. She returned to Mrs. Dix's home and vowed that she would never go home again. William sent her an agitated letter from Blue Mountain Lake later that month, on September 26, in which he said, "it has been more of less a hobby of yours to be considered a martyr." He warned that if she refused to submit to their father, the "controller of your goings and comings," she would find herself with little money while their father lived and possibly nothing at all after his death. Ella later admitted that her father had "certainly said some very cross things," but she added that he took it all back afterwards and that William exaggerated the events of that summer for his own advantage.

William was as impetuous as his sister, but his behavior was tempered by the expectation that he would take over the family's affairs when their father died. He believed that he got little encouragement from his father and none from her. In 1883–1884, when he was about thirty-three (**Fig. 8**), he insisted on a raise in salary. He wanted to marry Janet Lathrop Stott, who, like him, had little money of her own. Dr. Durant refused, saying he had no money to give, to which William replied that he would go to Texas, having "made arrangements to go as a cowboy or anything else." Mrs. Durant interceded and gave the couple sufficient cash, about $3,500, to marry. The wedding gift was given to Janet, not William. Thus the couple was launched on married life with the husband nominally in debt to his wife.

William and Janet were married on October 15, 1884 and settled down at a house at 167 Union Avenue in Saratoga Springs, a convenient location between his Adirondack activities to the north and those to the south, in Albany and New York City. The marriage was partly one of convenience, since the Stotts, Durants and Lathrops had business and marriage ties dating back to the second quarter of the century. Janet's middle name was Lathrop, a family which had moved its shipping interest from Lake Champlain to the Hudson River and married with the Stott family, owners of a textile mill in Columbia County south of Albany. Dr. Durant, her father-in-law, had gotten his start in business in the 1840's as a partner in the grain shipping firm of Durant, Lathrop and Company. William and Janet, who were thirty-four and nineteen years of age in 1884, perhaps followed a precedent within the three families for consolidating their fortunes through marriage. On March 8, 1885, Dr. Durant raised William's salary to $175 a month, and eventually they had two servants and a nurse for the first of their three children.

Dr. Durant was seriously ill following an operation for pleurisy in the summer of 1883. Not expected to live, he was returned to the North Creek house where two doctors, brought up on the train, tended the surgical wound in his chest. They taught Ella to change his dressings. She had a friend, Frances Murphy, staying with her those grim months.

William acted quickly. He directed the goings and comings of the physicians and installed a telegraph in the house so he might communicate with them in Saratoga Springs. He had the title to the house recorded at the Warren County clerk's office in his mother's name. Other deeds were probably recorded at this time.

The culmination of this drama took place one day when a special train arrived in North

Creek carrying Dr. Durant's business associates and relatives. His brother Charles and nephew Howard were in the party. John Barbour, the doctor's attorney in Saratoga, was in the group, along with Gen. Silas Seymour, a civil engineer, and Mr. C. E. Durkee, who later was superintendent of the railroad.

These men brought a document or two, the contents of which were never clearly identified at the trial in 1899. William had been trying to get his father to sign a will for some years without success, but the paper was more likely an option which Seymour, an associate during Dr. Durant's Union Pacific days, wanted on the railroad. Dr. Durant, maintaining he would regain his health, refused to sign anything and the group retired for tea where they solemnly discussed the doctor's unwillingness to cooperate.

Dr. Durant was astounded when the men were brought into his bedroom, and he exploded when they departed. He was so agitated that William had the train halted and the physician on board brought back. Dr. Durant saw William as the instigator of the mission and he rebuked his son for installing the telegraph and transferring title to the house. He may have discerned in William an unflattering readiness to seize authority at a moment of mortal vulnerability. The symptoms of ambition, which he had seen in others on numerous occasions, were evident in the son.

William had attempted to emulate his father's decisiveness, and, as had happened in less dramatic ways before, he was rebuffed. Entering a room occupied by Miss Murphy, he despondently told of his frustrations — he "had sacrificed his summer in order to be able to do his best for his father and his family," he said, only to be greeted by his father with "great coldness and at times great irritation."*

That winter, Dr. and Mrs. Durant lived in Florida. They received a copy of their daughter's book of poems, just published, and Mrs. Durant wrote to tell Ella how much they enjoyed it. The letter gave no indication that they felt the book was an accomplishment or that Ella should be encouraged to pursue her obvious craving for an independent life of her own.

Dr. Durant began sinking on the evening of October 5, 1885. Word went out to his wife and daughter, who were at Blue Mountain Lake and Raquette Lake. William ordered a special train which left Saratoga Springs, according to the *Delaware & Hudson Bulletin* for July 1, 1929, at 8:03 and delivered him in North Creek, near the doctor's residence, in 54 minutes. The average speed was 63.522 miles per hour. A railroad historian said this undoubtedly was the fastest time ever made on the Adirondack Railroad.

Dr. Durant died at 3:37 a.m. the next day. On the day of the funeral, which took place at the house on October 8, John Barbour arrived carrying two documents assigning power of attorney to William from his mother and sister. Mrs. Durant, in her bed, signed one. Ella was called into the room and her mother asked her to sign the other. Dr. Durant had died without a will, and William would need authority to carry on negotiations for the sale of the Adirondack Railroad and its properties. William assured his sister that the estate was worth about $1½ million and that it would be divided equally among the three of them. Ella refused, at least at first. Old hostility between the sister and brother surfaced. Privately she told Barbour downstairs that she had "no confidence in her brother, that she knew he would cheat and rob her if he got the chance." She wanted to hire a lawyer of her own. She eventually signed power of attorney to her brother, though the exact date this occurred is not clear.

After the service in North Creek, the doctor's remains were taken in a coach draped in

---

*Of Miss Murphy, William testified, "She may be mistaken; she is a woman."

black to Brooklyn where they were interred in the family's mausoleum in Green Wood Cemetery (Fig. 26). In New York, William helped his sister purchase a ticket on a boat bound for England. She had been contemplating a trip abroad for some months, but her haste in following through with these plans betrays her own exhilaration with her newly won freedom. Ella sailed out of New York harbor on October 20, fourteen days after her father's death. It would be nearly seven years before she returned, to find her financial affairs, unlike those of her brother and mother, very much unchanged.

His father no longer an obstacle, William moved with alacrity. The day after his father's death, he submitted a petition in Surrogate's Court for appointment as administrator of the estate. A few days later, $98,108 in claims against the estate were being bought up by William Sutphen, Dr. Durant's attorney in New York City. Some of the claimants accepted amounts less than owed them. The silent purchaser of these "judgments" against the estate was Janet L. Durant, who became nominal holder of $98,108 in claims against the estate for perhaps as little as a third of that amount. The money for these purchases came from William as administrator of the estate.

Secretive even with his family, Dr. Durant departed this world intestate, leaving behind bundles of stocks, bonds and mortages which made unclear assignments to the family members and business associates. The estate's size will probably always be uncertain. Much of Dr. Durant's property existed on paper and was subject to challenge by the state and possibly others as well. In 1899, Heloise's lawyers forced William to give them the financial records of the estate as it existed in 1885. Besides showing that William had a meager bank account of $17 at the time of his father's death, the attorneys described the estate as follows: 1) 400,000 acres of lands in the Adirondacks, 2) stocks and bonds of the Adirondack Railway Company, 3) two mortgages worth $150,000 apiece. The securities probably included additional land, perhaps as many as 240,000 acres.

Ella and the Sale 7

Within weeks of his father's death, William West Durant began looking for a buyer of the Adirondack Railway Company, of which he was the president and general manager. This was a continuation of efforts begun at least fourteen years earlier when Dr. Durant sought to find investors in London who would extend the road beyond its terminus near North Creek to Ogdensburg, N.Y., 125 miles to the north. Such a railroad would open up lands for agriculture, the development of timber, mineral and water resources, and it would likewise attract prosperous families seeking choice lakeside lots on which to build summer cottages easily reached by the marvelous convenience of the railroad.

In 1886, an option on the railroad was purchased by Edward Crane for $30,000. William offered to sell the company for $1,300,000 or, if the mortgages held by the company were excluded, for $1,100,000. It is not established whether Edward Crane was related to Dr. Durant's confidential clerk and the treasurer of the old Adirondack Company, Henry C. Crane, who built one of the first summer cottages on Blue Mountain Lake. Edward Crane failed to take up the option and he forfeited $30,000 to William that spring.

Yet another proposal was made in 1886. On December 8, the railroad and some 300,000 acres of its lands were offered to Daniel Odell, a broker in New York City, for $1,323,299. Odell declined, but he would later show William's written offer to Charles Henry Marcus Rose, the future husband of William's sister and an employee in Odell's office.

William was not short of money during this period of negotiation. He disposed of land and timber between February and November of 1886 for $135,647.12, a sum adequate to confer a patience and thoroughness to his search for a buyer of the railroad.

He sold the Adirondack Railway Company to the Delaware and Hudson Canal Company in June, 1889. We do not know how much cash was exchanged in this transacton. His checkbook at this time showed that he received $668,910.40 from the D&HCC (which, in 1829, had become the first railroad in the Western Hemisphere to operate a locomotive), but he also got additional sums for a quantity of Adirondack lands and two mortgages. The lands were sold to Chauncey Truax for $200,000 and the mortages carried face values totaling $300,000. Certainly it seems safe to say that William West Durant, acting as administrator of Dr. Durant's estate and as legal agent for his mother, sister and himself, enriched the family's cash worth by more than $1 million by the year's end.

In the months leading up to the sale, William struck up a friendship with Collis P. Huntington (1821–1900), a giant in the transportation and shipbuilding industries. Self-made and formerly Dr. Durant's counterpart in the construction of the western length of the transcontinental railroad in the 1860's, the aging Huntington allowed himself to be appointed a director of the Adirondack Railway Company while William was negotiating its sale. Huntington must have done this as a favor to William, who deserves credit for gaining Huntington's interest in the Adirondacks at the time that Huntington was about to dispose of his railroad holdings elsewhere in the United States. Before century's end William would find his future altogether dependent on Huntington's continued health and good will.

Heloise Hannah Durant was about 33 years old when she arrived by ship in England during the autumn of 1885. Ella was returning to a society she knew and liked. She and her brother had spent their youth travelling in Europe and staying with family and friends in England. At this time, Britain was at the pinnacle of its global power; and London, where Ella settled down, was the capital towards which cultivated people were drawn, like children to a toy store.

Darkly handsome (Fig. 11) but past the conventional age for marriage, Ella must have settled expectantly into her new surroundings. To acquaintances, she was heiress to the fortune left by a builder of America's first transcontinental railroad. But she was not another American woman looking for diversion and a secure marriage. Having published a book of poems, with other literary projects in progress, she possessed credentials as an intelligent and creative person in her own right.

There is little information about Ella's life at this time. An incident that occurred during a visit by her brother William and his wife Janet is suggestive. When William asked her to join them for dinner, she got his permission to bring a "Monsieur Berton" with her. William and Janet usually stayed at a fine London hotel, and Ella had an apartment or flat in South Kensington. As the conversation among the four progressed, it became apparent to William that his sister's companion was connected with the stage. Mr. Berton was the director of a theatrical company. It made little difference that the company was amateur, since stiff-necked Victorians, however much they might occasionally enjoy seeing a play from the auditorium, were convinced that wicked things happened behind the curtain once it dropped and the performers and their admirers were left to their own devices. Perhaps Ella intended to expose her brother's own excitable nature behind his stiff demeanor. He expressed his anger, she later said, by not seeing her home, allowing M. Berton to accompany her in the carriage instead.

In the summer of 1889, she met Arthur B. Frethey, an impecunious medical student who may not have gotten his degree. They were married at the Anglican church in Bexhill, overlooking the English Channel, on July 13, 1891. No member of Ella's family attended the wedding, though she received a wedding gift of five hundred dollars from her mother. Frethey had no job, and the state of his health is suggested by the medical attention he required before his death in Bexhill on August 29, just six weeks after the marriage, at the age of twenty-seven.

Ella received a monthly allowance of $200 in 1890–94. Still, she found herself short of money to pay bills for doctor and nursing care for herself and her late husband. When William presented her with a bill for her share of repairs to the family mausoleum in Green Wood Cemetery, built in 1873 at a cost of $60,000, she said she could not pay it and agreed when he offered to repair the tomb himself and buy her rights to it for $1,000.

Ella had misgivings for her share of the estate left by Dr. Durant to his wife and two children. Within a year of her arrival in London she spoke to the first of several lawyers about revoking the power of attorney she had signed over to her brother. William replied sarcastically to these discreet overtures and refused to cooperate. Arrayed against her were her mother, her mother's companion Miss Molineaux and John Barbour, each of whom chided her in letters for lacking confidence in her brother. Barbour wrote that claims were held against the estate, principally a judgment for $20 million obtained years earlier by a group of Rhode Island investors against Dr. Durant for losses resulting from the collapse of the Crèdit Mobilier in 1871. This judgment alone, he wrote on April 14, 1887, would wipe out the estate.

Not to be put off, she continued to inquire about her affairs, without success except perhaps for the irritation it caused William, who felt she was maligning him. In the summer of 1889, a month or so after the sale of the Adirondack Company to the Delaware and Hudson Canal Company, he arrived in London with his wife and gave Ella nearly £5,000. This, he said, was her portion of the estate.

In today's dollars, Ella was richer by more than $80,000, but the sum was far less than the one-third share she expected from the estate. She said to William that she had heard that their father's railroad had been sold:

". . . I asked him then where the money was that he told me the third of which would come to me . . . and he told me I didn't understand business. . . . [Then I] asked him where he got his money from. He said it was none of my business. I asked him where mother got hers . . . and he said he refused to divulge the affairs of his client. And then I asked him where my money came from that mother sent me, and he said that also was none of my business. I said, 'You know that you had no money before father died, and mother neither,' and that is how I came to say, 'How did you and mother get your money?' "

Later, at dinner, Ella pursued the matter, saying she ". . . could not understand how it was possible that there was no money realized out of all that railroad." At this William "became extremely angry . . . and struck the table so the champagne glasses jumped up, and he shook his fist, and said if I was a man he would shoot me, 'because you imply a doubt in my integrity.' " Janet exclaimed "Will!," and put her hand on her husband's arm, at which he turned on her and said, " 'You are my wife, your rooms are around the corner; go and stay there.' "

The hostility between William and his sister had been planted long before the death of their father. The origin cannot be known, but it may have grown out of competition for the favor of their father, on whom they were totally dependent until they were well into their adult years. We may admire Ella and see her as a forerunner of today's modern woman, striving for a larger measure of freedom and achievement than was tolerable to most men and women of her class at the time. In the final analysis, she was a poor manager of her affairs, admitting at one point to a tendency to "drift around," an aimlessness understandable since if followed the pattern she had known since childhood. She lost most of the money that her brother turned over to her in 1889. Amounting to $24,226, she said she donated about $1,500 of it to hospitals and missions in England; a far larger portion, perhaps as much as $20,000, was turned over to a "Count LaSalle," who invested it in a business venture which later failed.

If anything was certain to arouse Ella and raise the eyebrows of her friends in New York, it was the luxurious yacht, powered by steam and sail, which William commissioned in July, 1890 from the Philadelphia shipbuilding firm of Neafie & Levy, which received $108,000 from him in 1890–91 (Fig. 19). According to Harold Hochschild, in *Township 34*, the *Utowana* cost more than $200,000 to build and outfit. The design, furnishings and supervision were by John Beavor Webb, an Irish-born yacht architect who established a successful business in New York City following his arrival in the city in 1885. He also designed J. Pierpont Morgan's second and third Corsair yachts in 1890 and 1899. The maiden arrival of William's 191-foot ship in New York harbor was followed by an effusive full-page picture story in the April 19, 1891 issue of *The New York Times*.

William West Durant, elected a member of the New York Yacht Club (he would belong to others) on October 23, 1890, daringly claimed his place among America's elite by virtue of his ownership of the ultimate symbol of Victorian wealth, an ocean-going ship with a uniformed crew. When J. P. Morgan was asked how much it cost to own a yacht, he replied, "If you have to ask, you can't afford it." According to Hochschild, various members of Europe's nobility, including the future King Edward VII, were entertained on board the *Utowana*.

William crossed the Atlantic twice in 1891 and 1892, leaving his ship the first voyage to visit Ella at her South Kensington home where he threatened to cut off her allowance if she continued to inquire about his affairs. Widowed, uncertain and angry, Ella decided to do what she must have known was inevitable, return to the United States. William was on his second voyage, a prolonged one which took him to London, Madeira and other ports, when she crossed the Atlantic, arriving in New York in September, 1892 after an absence of seven years.

Point of No Return

8

After her arrival in New York, Ella visited with relatives in Albany, then returned to the city where she contacted a family friend and one of the city's most admired citizens, Abram S. Hewitt, a philanthropist who had served as a Congressman in 1874–87 and a reform mayor in 1887–89. He agreed to act as a peace-maker and wrote a latter which William received soon after returning from a two month cruise aboard the *Utowana*.

William respectfully declined Hewitt's offer to mediate the dispute, enclosing with his reply a check for $500, which he suggested be used to hire a reputable attorney who could assess the circumstances without bias. The 70-year-old Hewitt was angered by William's ignoring personal responsibilities in preference for seeing the conflict as a matter best left to lawyers and accountants, as symbolized by the check, which Hewitt caustically referred to as William's "certificate of character." Hewitt returned the check, and his answer expressed a view that would come to be widely held in the years immediately ahead. "Under no circumstances," he wrote on November 11, 1892, "would I leave a member of my own family in the position in which your sister is placed. Her eccentricities would not in any way change the obligation, which I should feel, to place her in an independent position."

William, perhaps stung by this, wrote Hewitt on December 22, 1892, saying that he would create a trust fund for his sister "within a reasonable time," but that he still desired that a "disinterested and honourable person should ascertain the falsehood of my sister's most unjust and cruel aspersions against my character." At least two other individuals were to make similar overtures on William's behalf to her. Verplanck Colvin, the State Surveyor and an acquaintance, approached her; also Robert DeForest, a prominent attorney and visitor to Camp Pine Knot, who intimated in 1894 that William would "make some pecuniary provision" for her.

Impatient, Ella hired a lawyer who tried, unsuccessfully, to serve William with a summons in the Adirondacks in February, 1893. She dismissed him soon after. The following December, C. W. Cotterill wrote her brother a letter which delicately proposed, ". . . investigations seem to indicate that you have a larger interest than was at first supposed."

It was a year and a half later, on June 18, 1895, that the law firm of Parsons, Shepard & Ogden submitted a complaint on behalf of Heloise H. Frethey. It asked "judgment that the defendant may be compelled fully to account" to his sister with respect to money and property obtained and disposed of since the death of Dr. Thomas Clark Durant on October 5, 1885. A summons was issued that day which required an answer from William West Durant within twenty days of its service.

William's attorney in this action was Joseph H. Choate, a respected and familiar social and political figure who would be appointed ambassador to Britain in 1899. Choate managed to delay things for his client. A countersuit was attempted and at one point Choate was considering an appeal for dismissal on grounds of the statute of limitations. William later said he rejected the latter route since it would not have cleared his name.

Eighteen months later the suit was dismissed as a "non-suit" on technical grounds, but this decision, dated December 16, 1896, was reversed on appeal and a new trial was ordered. Delays again occurred and months passed before the trial began. When it did, on January 5, 1899, the court room was filled with an audience of friends and onlookers. Thousands of readers were tantalized by daily newspaper accounts of a brother and sister of a socially prominent family pitted against one another.

It is not known how Ella supported herself and found money to hire lawyers for her case. She had continued to receive monthly checks until 1894, when they were halved to $100. By the spring of 1895, when a complaint was being prepared on her behalf, they stopped altogether. She had friends who might very well have been willing to lend support.

Ella remarried on August 31, 1895. Charles H. M. Rose was a clerk for Daniel Odell, a broker who had handled land transactions for Dr. Durant and whom William had approached as a potential buyer of the Adirondack Railway Company. Perhaps Ella and Rose had been introduced to one another by Odell. Ella's mother did not attend the wedding. Staying in California in 1895, she received few if any of the letters which Ella sent to be forwarded from William's office in New York, not even the one, dated January 31, 1896, which described her marriage and the expected arrival of a baby in the spring. Then about forty-two, Ella wrote, "it is rather late in life for me to be starting a family," adding that if the baby survived her "you must remember that it is your own grandchild." Mrs. Durant's companion, Miss Molineaux, later testified that she had been intercepting Ella's correspondence for some years and selecting which letters would be shown to Mrs. Durant and which would not. She had also sent copies to William. Ella and her son, Timbrell, who was born in New York City on May 6, 1896, were shown together in the photograph that accompanied a story in the *New-York Daily Tribune* about her suit against her brother (Fig. 22).

*   *   *

If there was a time when William West Durant might have altered the future course of events, it could be said to have been in 1895. Early that year he lured Collis P. Huntington to the Adirondacks by selling Camp Pine Knot to the transportation titan and gaining an ally and a creditor. He stopped sending the monthly allowance to his sister in the spring, and on October 12 he incorporated the Forest Park and Land Company (FP&LC), thus securing many of the lands originally owned by the old Adirondack Company from his sister and possibly his wife as well. By year's end there was no turning back. He would defy his sister and rely on Huntington's support for developing his Adirondack properties.

The land company was William's response to the complaint which Ella lodged against him in June, in which she asked the court for an accounting of her brother's handling of the estate since their father's death in 1885. The bulk of the new company's lands had belonged to the Adirondack Company. The rest, perhaps 56,000 acres, was owned by William, although he later admitted that some might once have been the Adirondack Company's. Several of the subscribers to the FP&LC were members of the Durant family or friends and associates loyal to William. Dr. Arpad Gerster took $125,000 in stock in exchange for 27,000 acres of land in Hamilton County. Henry "Commodore" Bradley, who ran Durant's transportation system and later managed land sales for him, received $150,000 in stock for 34,000 acres of land in Hamilton and Franklin Counties, subject to a $71,000 mortgage held by William's mother. William, who was president of the company, at an annual salary of $20,000, took $22,500 in stock for tracts in Hamilton, Franklin and Essex Counties, plus water rights in Franklin, Essex and St. Lawrence Counties.

It is likely that little or no cash was involved in this transaction. The lands were probably deeded by William or their nominal owners to these individuals, who deeded them back to the FP&LC. Separating appearance from reality is difficult, for William often used other people as a cover in the acquisition of land. This tactic dated back to Dr. Durant's time. Sorting out the transfers of property was a difficult task for Ella and her attorneys, who were sustained by the simple fact that William was nearly penniless in 1885 but was living like a millionaire in 1890. Most of the papers left at Dr. Durant's death, described as "enormous in quantity," would not be accounted for at the time of the trial.

As if his affairs were not sufficiently tangled, William also had to contend with other lawsuits at this time. He initiated a suit for divorce against Janet in 1896, naming Dr. Richmond Pratt, her doctor, as co-respondent. The court held this was not established and denied William's suit. A story in *The New York Times* for August 9, 1898 reported that Janet had obtained a divorce, custody of their three children and an assessment of $5,950 in costs. She also was suing him to recover lands in Hamilton County that he had, with power of attorney, disposed of for her. William's lawyer in this action was Joseph H. Choate, who later brought suit of his own against his former client, with unknown results. Janet was represented by Elihu Root and later by Richard W. DeForest.

The couple may have been all but separated by 1894, when a visitor at Camp Pine Knot observed that William was living on the houseboat while Janet was spending the night at the Durant Cottage at Pine Knot. Years later, Maurice Callahan, who was then the telegraph operator at the camp, recalled that William spent most of the summer of 1895 at Camp Uncas, that he was seen but once or twice at Pine Knot where Janet was staying, and that she did not visit Uncas..

Ella watched her brother's predicament with growing apprehension. She knew of the formation of the Forest Park and Land Company and of the sales of lands to Huntington, Morgan and Woodruff, and she was certain that these and other lands being disposed of by her brother had originally belonged to the Adirondack Company and its successor, the Adirondack Railway Company. The separation of William and Janet raised a complicating factor about the terms of a settlement should Janet win her suit. Sure enough, in October, 1897, Janet filed a *lins pendens* suit claiming a dower right to the $167,107 condemnation price which the state agreed to pay for 23,872 acres of Durant lands in Township 6. The state decided it could not withhold purchase money in a condemnation proceeding, and William was paid.

A former employee of William's came to Ella during the spring of 1898 and said that William was planning to flee the country for England. By this time, William had negotiated a divorce settlement with his wife, but the retrial of his sister's suit was still pending. Ella informed her lawyers, who on June 24, 1898 obtained a warrant for his arrest. He was taken into custody in July, and was released only after posting bond of $10,000. Collis P. Huntington loaned the money to William, who repaid it the following March.

The arrival of Collis P. Huntington (Fig. 31) in the Adirondacks was accomplished largely through Durant's efforts. The two were friendly. Huntington occasionally left notes at William's hotel in the city, asking for William or inviting him to join him and Mrs. Huntington for dinner. William carried a case of Maderia wine aboard the Utowana for Huntington, and he placed Camp Pine Knot at Huntington's disposal in 1890. In his letter of thanks, on stationery of the Southern Pacific Railway, Huntington said he was indebted to William for "the pleasantest experience of 'roughing it' in camp that it was ever my fortune to get, and Mrs. Huntington joins me in saying that nobody but Mr. and Mrs. Durant could have made the hospitality so unique and acceptable." Nearly five years later, the camp, its furnishings and two hundred acres were sold to Huntington for $35,000, a low price when one examines the inventory of contents and accepts William's later estimate that he had spent $75,000 on the camp before its sale.

Thomas Clark Durant and Huntington were similar in many respects. Except for education — Huntington dropped out of school to fend for himself, while Thomas Durant was graduated from medical school at the early age of twenty — the two shared similar backgrounds. Both were born in New England at about the same time, got their foothold in business in upstate New York and both got into railroading, to meet, eventually, in the construction of the transcontinental railroad, in which they collaborated for their respective railroad companies, the Union Pacific and Central Pacific railroads. They were physically large, quickly dominated those around them and were accustomed to wielding power.

Perhaps William had learned from dealing with his father how to ingratiate himself with a man such as Huntington, who, for his part, having no natural children of his own, appreciated William's attentions and spunk. Having been the target of public criticism for most of his life, Huntington may have felt sympathetic as William became drawn into a succession of troublesome lawsuits.

By December of 1899, Huntington held two mortgages on the Forest Park and Land Company for $100,000 apiece. One mortage, dated August 15, 1898, had passed to him from Joseph P. Lloyd, and the other, dated December 15, 1899, was made out to Huntington. That year, William pressed Huntington for cash, asking for $12,000 on December 28, 1899 and "at least" $15,000 on February 13, 1900. The latter loan, William said, could be deducted from the price of the Arbutus Lake camp and preserve. Little wonder that Huntington insisted on Durant providing him with a breakdown on all of the properties held by the Forest Park and Land Company. Besides these debts to Huntington, William owed $47,000 to other parties, who held his transportation line as security.

Collis P. Huntington thus became Durant's chief creditor. Friendship and confidence were reciprocated between the two, though Huntington always made sure that his loans were safely secured by William's properties. On April 12, 1897, Huntington wrote his brother-in-law and private secretary, Isaac Edwin Gates, whom Huntington addressed as "Brother Gates," concerning a loan of $40,000 to Durant. Huntington wrote, "I would, of course, rather not let him have the money, for, as you know every well, I have no money to lend, and I do this only to help him out. But if the title is good, the security is unquestioned and I think good for a very much larger sum than forty thousand dollars."

"The Finest Trio"   9
Camps Uncas,
Sagamore and Kill Kare

On January 3, 1893, near the end of their holiday visit to Camp Pine Knot, a party of Durant and Stott family members accompanied William West Durant in sleighs over the ice and snow to Mohegan Lake where they enjoyed a picnic in the "snowy forest," walked in snow shoes on the lake and watched as William selected a site for Camp Uncas. This territory, south of Raquette Lake and encompassing all of Township 5 and part of Township 6, was untouched except for trails and two cabins which William built in the 1880's on Sumner and Shedd Lakes [later Kora and Sagamore Lakes] as retreats for friends and acquaintances, including Governor Black and other officials, who eagerly took advantage of William's invitation to hunt and fish there and in the fine grounds farther south, near the Moose River. Between 1893 and 1897 William would carve out three large preserves of 1,000 to 1,500 acres apiece, and at the edge of the lake of each would be built a camp, Uncas, Sagamore and Kill Kare, described in 1903 by an English writer as "the finest trio on the North American Continent." Already known for Pine Knot, William's later reputation as the creator of the "Camp Beautiful" was derived from these camps.

William set the pattern for these camps and their emulators elsewhere in the Adirondacks, but the fragmentary record indicates that they were smaller, more intimate and nearer to the wilds when he was running things, down to about 1902, than in later years. In 1901 William said that Sagamore could be staffed by a superintendent and wife, a teamster and two laborers, at a monthly cost of $260 including board. Two horses, two cows, incidentals and taxes brought the estimated monthly cost, "without entertaining," to a grand total of $450. By the time of the First World War, the camps, particularly Sagamore and Kill Kare, had grown considerably.

Three of five children of Richard J. Collins, the superintendent at Sagamore until 1924, recall that Sagamore had approximately twenty resident staff and perhaps another fifteen who were personal servants of the owners. Guests numbered about thirty, as a rule, and up to fifty on occasion. Our notion of the grand camps as woodland palaces for the superich is colored by their later years.

But there is no question about the stylishness which William introduced to camp life, an intangible but essential quality which can be recollected by a dwindling few and imagined by the rest. In 1899 a clerk of the New York Senate, Mr. James S. Whipple, wrote the following account of the approach of a party of officials to Kill Kare (Fig. 97):

> We arrived at Camp Kill-Kare just at dark, and as we drove across the ice, on the stretch of lake lying between the highway where it approaches Lake Kora's shore near the camp, the bright lights hanging in many places among the trees about this beautiful woodland home of the [Lieutenant] Governor, flashed out their evening welcome. As we swung up to the door, the sleighbells jingling out their merry tunes, the guides received us taking the teams and helping us out of the sleigh. Inside the bright fires blazed from great stone fire-places, and the table was spread with all the delicacies one would expect to find at Delmonico's. . . .

97

The ends of the logs of the lodge were laid up "true as a die," and the "ceiling and walls inside polished with wax until one can see his face reflected therefrom as in a mirror." Rugs of bear, deer and fox skins were on the floors and animal trophies — marten, mink and otter and various birds — adorned the walls and shelves, along with "steel traps, knives, guns and implements of the chase." There were books on all subjects, mostly outdoor adventures, and the "furniture was all made from the native timber." Bathrooms with hot and cold running water left no doubt that "the Adirondack camp of the rich man today would make a well-to-do suburbanite envious to have it for his own home."

In 1903 a writer and traveller from England, Henry Wellington Wack, had the opportunity of comparing the three camps. He concluded:

> I suppose these three camps, thus situated on private lakes, connected with the rivers of the region by inlets and outlets; with trails carefully blazed in every direction; connecting each other by private roads and telephones, with driveways to Raquette Lake, to Old Forge and the Fulton Chain [of Lakes], with two hundred thousand acres of State forest preserve all around them . . . constitute in cost and comfort, in pleasurable appointments and luxury, the finest trio on the North American Continent. And I doubt if there is any forest villa in Europe to compare with either of them in any respect.

Elsewhere Wack said that seventy guests could be housed at Kill Kare, a plausible enough number after the reconstruction and enlargement of Kill Kare by the Garvan family about 1916, but possibly exceeding the camp's capacity in 1903.

Life at the camps was two-fold, divided between the staff and the owners and their guests. Crucial to the happiness and smooth running of a camp was the superintendent and his wife. Responsibility for the entire camp complex was in the hands of the superintendent, whose authority was exceeded only by the owner, his family or, when the family was in residence, perhaps by a personal secretary.

The camps were located within several miles of one another and there was an ongoing exchange of men among the three. John and Mary Callahan worked for Durant and then for the Morgans at Camp Uncas until about 1920, at which time their son, Thomas, replaced them until he assumed the superintendent's job at Sagamore in 1924. The Callahans were cooks, but Mary's culinary reputation, gained partly by Durant's instruction, was known far and wide. J. Pierpont Morgan asked William to let them remain at Uncas, and William, who had employed them since 1889, reluctantly complied. Morgan and his guests so seldom visited the camp during the first years that William, on April 30, 1900, inquired into Morgan's plans that summer: "John and Mary Callahan do not want to stay there another summer unless some of the family do occupy it. It seems too lonely for them, and besides, Mary gets out of practice in having no one to cook for except a laborer or so. . . ."

Sagamore had the largest staff of the three camps. Richard J. Collins was superintendent from about 1897 to 1924, at which time he left to operate a hotel, the former Duryea camp, in Blue Mountain Lake. Margaret, his wife, was half-sister to John Callahan at Uncas. The Collins children, who provided information for this book, attended class in an "annex" at Sagamore and observed the personalities who passed through the isolated camp on Sagamore Lake. Workmen whom they recalled at Sagamore at various times give an idea of the variety of jobs at Sagamore:

Carpenters: Garry Rogers, Josh Smith, Freeland Jones and Albert Roblee.
Painter: Frank Little.
Blacksmith: Charles Dougherty, James Leffler.
Stableman: Fred Wallace.

98

Electrician (starting c. 1915) *and wife:* W.C.M. Ryan.
Chores and general work: Frank Owens, George Wright, Francis Pirong, Dave Davis.
Masons: Schuyler Kathan, Frank Flynn and George Starbuck.
Line watchman (game warden): Joe Smith.
Guide: Fred "Mossy" Maxam.
Teamster: Hank Burnham, Douglas Millington, Johnny Hoy.
Gardner: George Wilson and a man named Hayes.

Mrs. Hoy, a cook in the men's house, was widowed about 1915 when a tree fell on a carriage driven by her husband. Many of the men were unmarried, and some worked seasonally or as needed. The carpenters, painter, perhaps the blacksmith Dougherty, and the stone mason Kathan had been employed by William West Durant on these and other projects prior to the turn of the century. The craftsmanship of the Durant camps and their furnishings is likely due to these men.

The Vanderbilts came to Sagamore with a retinue of their own, among which might be a secretary, valet, chef, assistant chef, butler, chamber maid, laundress, footman, horse-man, governess and nurse. Kamp Kill Kare had a staff almost as large. An insurance report in 1930 reported that the Garvan place had ten to twelve employees in winter and thirty to forty in summer.

One of the unanswered mysteries that has descended to the present time is the formula for the stain which Frank Little used on the woodwork at William West Durant's camps. That this was a problem is shown by a letter of February 8, 1902 to Durant from Edward Burns, the manager of Ne-Ha-Sa-Ne Park, who asked William to authorize Cottier & Company, a manufacturer of furniture and woodwork in New York, to sell four to six gallons of red and dark brown stains to Mr. Vanderbilt at Sagamore Lodge. Josh Smith, who was in charge of work at Sagamore, needed the stain for furniture and the "new building," but Cottier refused to comply without a letter from William. Wax, perhaps beeswax for its delicate scent, was applied to the stained woodwork. On June 29, 1899, William wrote John Callahan at Sagamore Lodge asking to have an extra bedstead made: "Frank Little can slip over some evening and stain it, and then [stain it] again and wax it. . . ." At the time Little was staining a room for Huntington at Camp Pine Knot.

The grand camps of the wealthy in the Adirondacks attracted a number of admiring journalists at the turn of the century, among them William Frederick Dix, editor of *Town and Country* magazine. Writing in *The Independent* in July, 1903, he said, "An Adirondack camp does not mean a canvas tent or a bark wigwam, but a permanent summer home where the fortunate owners assemble for several weeks each year and live in perfect comfort and even luxury, tho in the heart of the woods, with no very near neighbors, no roads and no danger of intrusion." The development of "the cottage idea" had, he noted, flourished for only a decade or so, but despite its newness, "it is an interesting phase of American social life and decidedly significant," by which he meant the turn toward "more simplicity for the vacation" and the united efforts of wealthy preserve owners and the state to protect the woods, waters and wildlife of the Adirondacks for future generations. The heyday of the grand camps is all but finished; Dix perhaps did not realize how brief their "significant phase" would be, about sixty years, and while it is difficult for us to see simplicity in woodland communities with a dozen or so employees, his remark about the camps as outposts guarding the Adirondack environment accurately describes the stewardship role their owners performed in later decades.

Camp Uncas

Taking its name from the young Indian chief in the novel by James Fenimore Cooper, *The Last of the Mohicans*, Uncas was built on a point of land on Mohegan Lake between 1893 and 1895. Except for occasional trips to Pine Knot or his floating "Barque" on Raquette Lake, William remained at Uncas supervising construction most of those summers. By the late summer of 1895, Uncas was sufficiently completed for Dr. Arapad Gerster to note in his journal, "Mr. D's luxurious camp is as beautiful as ever." The camp and its 1,500 acre preserve were sold the next year to J. Pierpont Morgan, the financier whose wealth enabled him to raise $65,000,000 in gold for the U.S. Treasury from banks in America, England and Europe. The property's selling price is not known, but in 1900 William told Seneca Ray Stoddard that Uncas had cost $120,000 before it was sold. It is possible that William owed money to Morgan and that the finished camp was part of an arrangement between the two men. William had told Huntington in 1895 that he needed to sell Pine Knot to cover his expenses at Uncas.

Uncas departed in scale and character from William's other camps. For one thing, the Uncas preserve enclosed a private lake and more land than had been previously set aside in the region for any single party's exclusive pleasure. This required the cutting of a road from South Inlet of Raquette Lake to Uncas in 1895 and from Uncas to Eagle Bay, a distance of 8½ miles, in 1896 (**Fig. 32**). Both Morgan and Huntington seem to have insisted on the road, which connected their camps with the railroad station at Clearwater. Morgan would not risk being without means of an overnight return to New York City in the event of some financial crisis. Later, when Raquette Lake had its own rail service, he kept a locomotive under steam 24 hours a day so he could be off without delay. A third road, connecting with the other two, was being cut from Sagamore to Kill Kare in September, 1897. A visitor to Kill Kare two years later said in an article in the *Albany Argus* that the 15 mile system of roads had cost $35,000 and that Durant, Morgan, Huntington and Woodruff had shared in the expense.

Another new feature was that Uncas was designed, built and furnished as an ensemble from start to finish. The other Durant camps evolved over a period of years and therefore reflected the eccentricities of time, temperament and the limited extent of land on which they were built. The imposition of a unified style, at least in the Manor House, is evidence that William was assisted by a professional architect or designer, possibly Grosvenor Atterbury (1869–1956), a visitor at Camp Pine Knot on April 5, 1893, or John Beavor Webb (1849–1927), the designer of William's yacht *Utowana* in 1890. A watercolor design for a desk and bookcase in the living room at Uncas (**Fig. 77**) bears William's name and that of Atterbury, the architect of the Long Island home of Robert DeForest, a friend of Durant's and a visitor to Pine Knot. Beavor Webb's role is less certain. He designed two of Morgan's Corsair yachts and was said to be ready to join Morgan on a cruise at a moment's notice. On July 6, 1899, William wrote the caretaker at Uncas, John Callahan, saying that no one was to see Uncas without orders from Mr. Morgan or from Mr. Morgan "through Mr. J. Beavor Webb or myself." It is tempting though risky to see a ship designer's hand in the window seats and tidy compartmentalization at Uncas. Comparison with the "dining saloon" of the *Utowana* is invited (**Figs. 21, 76**). Another architect with whom William had likely contacts in the 1890's was William L. Coulter (c. 1865–1907), who moved to Saranac Lake for his health about 1895. R. Newton Brezee (d. 1929), in practice in Saratoga Springs by 1888, made working plans in 1899 and 1900 from William's designs of cottages and fireplaces.

The Manor House was a two-story house on a raised basement of native stone with walls of spruce logs and a broad shingle roof with shed dormers (Fig. 75). Below and nearer Mohegan Lake were two log cottages, called Chingachgook (Fig. 80) and Hawkeye after Uncas's father and Natty Bumpo. The dining building was located about a minute's walk from the house, on a location overlooking the water and hills beyond (Fig. 79). This facility actually consisted of a cluster of connected and semi-attached structures, beginning with the dining room and followed by a pantry, kitchen, laundry, storerooms, shed and an ice house with two coolers. The superintendent's house was behind the kitchen and looked out on a lagoon of the lake. These service buildings were covered with cedar and spruce bark and trim, and they resembled the buildings that William built at Sagamore in 1897–1900. Other structures on the point at Uncas were a greenhouse, root cellar, pump house, lean-to and boat shed.

The farm buildings were located out of sight but not far distant from the Manor House. These consisted of a large house with about ten rooms for employees, a blacksmith's shop, two barns for cows, horses and pigs, and a large carriage house and shed. A summer pasture and perhaps garden were located on the east side of the lake.

The placement of the buildings on raised stone basements lent an architectural character not found at other camps to this time. The basements also provided space for coal and wood burning furnaces, enabling the buildings to be occupied the year round, a novel idea to Americans who still thought of the second home as a place to which one went in the summer. William was determined to show that the Adirondacks could be enjoyed in comfort every month of the year.

The log cottages at Uncas were not original, but the Manor House, as it later came to be called, was very much in the mainstream of current architectural practice, combining elements of two related and overlapping styles, the Queen Anne and Shingle Styles. The horizontal silhouette, deep verandah (on the front) and broad expanse of shingle roof denote the features of what only recently has come to be called the Shingle Style, but what an earlier generation referred to as a "free classic style." At the Manor House these features were more compact or less attenuated and exaggerated. The exemplar of the Shingle Style was the lodge designed by Robert Robertson and built for Dr. and Mrs. William Seward Webb at Na-Ha-Sa-Ne on Lake Lila at about the same time that the Manor House was going up at Uncas. The interior of the Manor House reflected Queen Anne elements, such as contrasting materials, casement windows, and beamed ceilings, and, above all, an open floor plan that enabled spaces to be divided into rooms and passageways of varying size. Pine Knot and the other camps discussed in a previous chapter adopted Queen Anne elements, but this was a decorative rather than a structural adoption. The earlier camps retained their log cabin heritage of small one and two room buildings. The tactic of applying such things as bay windows or of attaching one building to another could not obscure the primitive origins of Pine Knot.

The open plan is evident on both floors of the Manor House, particularly in the living rooms and its adjoining bedrooms where a system of giant posts, beams and joists, of white pine or spruce logs, broke up walls into alcoves, intimate nooks and small closets, and made possible rooms that were both more interesting and more spacious. This was no small step forward, as a comparison of the living room at Uncas (Fig. 76) with that at Camp Stott dramatically shows (Fig. 72). Peeled logs of this size, averaging sixteen inches in diameter, imparted a strongly masculine character to the rooms in the Manor House, recalling the advice of an English writer in the late 18th century, William Marshall, that the style of a hunting lodge be masculine throughout. Photographs of the suave log grid give a misleading impression of oppressively low ceilings. But the lowest members, the beams, saddle-notched on top to hold the log joists supporting the floor above, are eight feet from the floor, and the effects on occupants are of security and intimacy.

William's insistence on handsomely proportioned and executed stonework was continued at Uncas, where the fireplaces were larger and more original in conception than anything he had done before. For example, the mantel in the master bedroom was a peeled log cut in half along its length of almost twelve feet, about four feet of which extended beyond the fireplace on one side. It was supported by two stone brackets and peeled log posts (Fig. 78). The hearths at Uncas were raised several inches from the floor rather than being flush with it, as at Pine Knot.

Appearances to the contrary, the arrangement of rooms in the Manor House was simple: the living room in the central part, with a bedroom and bath on one side and a bedroom, bath and small room (today used as a kitchen) at the other end. Two small halls, with doors from the porch in front, were located between these three principal rooms, so a person entering the house could step into the living room or into an adjoining bedroom. The stairs were located in one of these halls. Fireplaces were in the two bedrooms. One of these was back-to-back with the fireplace in the living room (Figs. 76, 78). Upstairs there was a bedroom at each end, one with a fireplace. A large stair hall and what may have been a playroom occupied the center of this floor. Ample daylight was admitted to these rooms through the windows of shed dormers. These upstairs rooms were open to the roof, exposing the elaborate system of pole trusses, rafters and posts deemed necessary to assure that the roof would carry the heavy snows of winter and spring. There are two bathrooms, but one or both may have been added at a later date.

The furniture at Uncas was designed to be an unobtrusive part of the whole. A large number of beds and bureaus were required at Uncas, Sagamore and Kill Kare, and it is not surprising that furniture of similar design and construction was used at all three camps, indicating the exchange of ideas and workmen during the initial period of construction at the camps, 1893–1900. The quaint rustic furniture of William's early camps was discarded in favor of subdued pole and board furniture that was easy to produce and maintain. An innovative exception were the window seats that were adopted at Uncas and later at Sagamore and Kill Kare. Built under a window and sometimes L-shaped to fit into a corner, these had pine or spruce frames with curved armrests that may have been cut from the root of the spruce tree. Cushions of corduroy and pillows made these seats cozy gathering places within an otherwise large public room.

Durant was only partly responsible for the other building at Uncas which is held in particular esteem today, the dining hall. William's building was one story and oriented so its long side paralleled Mohegan Lake (Fig. 79). The present hall is far larger, 1½ stories high, with the end of the building facing the lake (Fig. 81). The source of this change was Miss Anne Morgan, one of Morgan's four children, who, according to a story in a Syracuse newspaper of June 13, 1954, was said to have directed the enlargement of the hall. Miss Morgan, perhaps assisted by an architect, raised the roof, turned it ninety degrees, placed a bedroom and bath above what had been William's dining area and created a new dining room, open to the rafters, with tall French doors framing a view of the lake and an enormous stone fireplace, twenty feet wide, which nearly filled the entire wall on one side (Fig. 82). The room was approximately square and had a ceiling that sloped on four sides, notwithstanding the simple gable roof outside. A circular wrought iron chandelier was suspended in the center of the room from a chain attached to the ridge pole. An iron plate fashioned as a compass enclosing the outline of a turtle, the totem of the clan to which Uncas belonged, held the chain to the ridge pole. The fireplace, exceeded in size only by one in the casino built about 1913 for Robert Collier at the camp formerly owned by the Stott family on Raquette Lake, was more decorative than functional, an ironic consequence, perhaps, of central heating which rendered smaller, more efficient fireplaces (and woodstoves) less necessary than before.

After J. Pierpont Morgan's death in 1913, Uncas passed to his children, who used it more frequently than had their father, according to Harold K. Hochschild in *Township 34.* Anne Morgan was an accomplished fisherman and hunter, as was her brother, J. P. "Jack" Morgan, who often was guided by Ollie Tuttle of Fourth Lake, the inventor and maker of "Tuttle Bugs" and other lures for fishing. In 1947, the Uncas estate was purchased by Mrs. Margaret Emerson, the widow of Alfred G. Vanderbilt and owner of Sagamore Lodge nearby. In 1953 she gave Uncas to a medical foundation, but by 1957 the property had been acquired by Uncas Estates, Inc., which opened it to the public as a museum and park. A picture story in *The New York Times* for August 21, 1966, said that Uncas had been sold the month before and that its future was "uncertain." Up to this point, Uncas had been little altered since the turn of the century. The apprehensions of a few people who wanted Uncas preserved in 1966 proved accurate, for the new owners, a trust acting on behalf of the Rockland County (N.Y.) Council of the Boy Scouts of America, failed to maintain the buildings and protect their contents. When this writer visited Uncas for the first time, in 1973, the Manor House had become a nearly-empty shell, an altogether different place than the completely finished woodland home depicted seven years earlier in *The Times.*

Uncas points up the plight of large camps in the Adirondacks. The institutions, charitable organizations and state agencies which acquire these properties, supplanting private for institutional patronage, are not as a rule prepared to give them the same dedicated attention. Money is part of the problem. In 1976 the maintenance of a large camp, according to its owner, was fifty to sixty thousand dollars. Part of the difficulty, however, has been the lack of commitment by organizations more concerned with the property's value as a future investment than with its worth as a place of civilized refuge.

Increasingly the state is looked to for help, but New York is mandated by law to remove man-made structures from lands acquired in the Forest Preserve. The solution arrived at by the state when Sagamore and Uncas were put up for sale in 1975 was to buy all of the lands but the seven and sixteen acres that contained the principal buildings at each camp. A buyer was sought who would give assurance that the camps would be cared for properly. Accordingly, Sagamore Lodge was sold to the National Humanistic Education Center, though not without Syracuse University, which had received Sagamore as a gift from Mrs. Emerson, auctioning many of the furnishings, a failure of stewardship if there ever was one. Drs. Howard and Barbara Glaser-Kirschenbaum, founders and directors of the Center, an organization dedicated to the examination of contemporary issues for adults and professionals, bought Camp Uncas, which they are restoring and which they use as a home when workshops require their attention at Sagamore. Aware of the formidable task ahead, the young couple managed to salvage some objects from the auction and they hope to obtain help which will enable the buildings at Sagamore to be restored to something of their former grandeur.

Sagamore

Having disposed of Camp Uncas, William turned his attention the next year to the start of a new camp complex on Sagamore Lake (formerly Shedd Lake) about two miles to the northeast. He also sold his yacht in 1897, which he seems not to have used much himself since his voyage abroad in 1893, to Allison V. Armour, a plant explorer. And he negotiated the sale that summer and fall of 23,872 acres in Township 6 to New York State and 1,030 acres of land around what came to be called Lake Kora (formerly Sumner Lake) to Timothy L. Woodruff, a Brooklyn Republican elected Lieutenant Governor in 1896. William presumably applied the money to the construction of Sagamore and to another camp which he began on Arbutus Lake in the spring of 1898. His business obligations and personal problems — his transportation system and costs arising from pending lawsuits by his wife and sister — continuously drained his resources, compelling him to turn more than once to Collis P. Huntington for additional financial assistance.

The land sales to New York and Woodruff were seen by the press as having a connection, though no actions were taken and an investigation in 1910 was inconclusive. At the time that Woodruff took possession of the preserve on August 27, 1897, the Forest Preserve Board, of which he was the chairman, was considering the purchase for the state of a far larger tract surrounding Uncas, Sagamore and Kill Kare. In July the Board met at Camp Uncas to inspect the land and discuss the price which the state should offer Durant for it. William wanted ten dollars an acre, but the Board eventually settled on seven dollars instead, only slightly higher than the per-acre price the state had paid for prime forest lands the year before. Before the state actually bought the tract in October, the Woodruffs had occupied the hunting camp on Lake Kora and were cutting a road to it.

A look at a map of the state's new acquisition (End Papers) showed the Lieutenant Governor in possession of a private in-holding entirely surrounded by Forest Preserve. Why, it was asked, had the Forest Preserve Board allowed 1,030 acres to be exempted from the condemnation proceedings? Blunting the force of any charge that a deal had been struck between Woodruff and Durant was the accepted view that the state had made a valuable addition to its holdings, and at an acceptable price. Another factor may have been the hunting and fishing camp which William and Dr. Gerster built on the lake in the 1880's. It constituted an "improvement" which could be difficult to wrest, that is, condemn, from an uncooperative owner.

An understanding must have been reached between Durant and Woodruff. The deed to the Kill Kare preserve was not recorded until February 14, 1898 and William would later feel no compunctions about going to Woodruff for special consideration in Albany, once writing the Lieutenant Governor, on December 29, 1899, "I want you to buy these [651 acres in Long Lake] for the State and to pay me a good price for them, which I think you ought to do, as you got the best of the bargain in the purchase of Township 6. . . ." Woodruff was instrumental in winning passage in 1899 of a law permitting an oil-fueled steam locomotive to operate on an eighteen mile length of track between Clearwater and Raquette Lake, and on one occasion he informed William that the Forest Preserve Board would offer $2,500 for titles to land which the Benedict family might claim. Thus armed, William was prepared to offer $5,000 for the titles. Woodruff, who aspired to the governorship (he lost the nomination in 1904), pointed out that his position in government did not allow him to perform personal favors. The state acquired the land on Long Lake, but for $3 an acre rather than the $4 that William had wanted.

Located at the northerly end of a triangle formed with Uncas and Kill Kare, Sagamore was the largest of the camps built by William in the Adirondacks. He wrote Stoddard on May 1, 1900, "It has cost me a great deal more than any of the other camps I have built, and is much more elaborate in the way of gas and water works, heating by furnace as well as by fireplaces, system of draining, roads and stocking the lake with fish, than anything I before attempted." Some of William's innovations, such as central heating, year-round water supply and sanitary sewage disposal had been introduced at Uncas, but his remark to the Glens Falls photographer indicates his particular pride with the engineering feats at Sagamore, most of which were buried or placed out of sight but constituted essential features which enabled these woodland communities to grow and accommodate, as they have done to the present day, up to a hundred or so occupants at a time. These conveniences impressed William's contemporaries who had recently begun to install them in their own homes in the city and were surprised when they found such things as heated bathrooms with hot running water, gas illumination and flush toilets (Fig. 93) in the heart of the Adirondack wilds.

William chose flat ground on a point of land at the western side of Sagamore Lake for the site of his camp. At the edge of the water he erected a lodge altogether unlike the one at Uncas and of such large proportions and assertiveness that one might conclude that he was inviting comparisons with Morgan's camp and with others on Raquette Lake nearby. Dr. Gerster visited Sagamore on May 11, 1898 and was duly impressed: "Durant's new building, erected in Swiss chalet style, constitutes a real ornament to the landscape." Measuring about twenty-seven by sixty-two feet, the lodge achieved its dominance by its height, three stories on a raised basement and piers of stone with the main entrance, a double door with wrought iron strap hinges and large studded nails, reached by three flights of stairs from the circular drive in front (Figs. 83, 91). Of frame construction overlaid with spruce slabs resembling logs, the lodge had two facades, both similar, with rustic verandahs on three levels, presenting the person approaching from either side, land or lake, with a formality not unlike that of Georgian houses on tidal rivers in the plantation South.

What the lodge gained in rustic monumentality on the outside, it lost in intimacy in the interior rooms, partly a consequence of the high ceilings which Durant perforce used, nearly ten feet on the first floor and eight and a half feet high on the second floor. James S. Whipple, the Clerk of the Senate, who was Durant's guest for Sunday dinner, described Sagamore as "more elaborate" and "much larger than the Lieutenant-Governor's, but not quite as unique and cozy." After dinner the group, which included Woodruff and two other members of the Forest Perserve Board, plus Senator Henry Marshall, sat "around the great fire-place smoking our cigars" as Alvah Dunning, the "oldest and best known guide in the Adirondacks," entertained them with stories about his experiences and observations in the region.

William probably designed all of the pre-1901 buildings at Sagamore. His ground plans for the camp, which are the basis for Figure 91, are among the Durant papers at the Adirondack Museum. His second wife, Annie Cotton Durant, claimed he was the architect of the chalet. A photograph of the living room, taken in 1899 by Seneca Ray Stoddard, shows a scale model of a Swiss chalet displayed on a table next to a photographic portrait taken of William about 1884 (Fig. 84). Possibly William used the model in some way in his design of the lodge. He was said to have showed a music box in the form of a Swiss chalet to the foreman of the crew that built a small Swiss style cottage for his use at Eagle Nest in 1900 (Fig. 35).

The main residences at Uncas and Sagamore were altogether different in style and feel, both outside and inside. The arrangement of rooms on the first floor was similar, a living room in the middle with a bedroom and bath on each side. The size and proportions of the chalet forced William, a gentleman architect, to fall back on the amateur's habit of filling large rectangles with smaller ones, a reversion to his Pine Knot years. As if to compensate, he created fireplaces of extraordinary design, bordering in a couple of instances on the bizarre. One of these (Fig. 85) was of the usual hewn stone, but an irregularly shaped recess above the arch was filled with red stucco in a fur-like pattern that converged toward the center. The mantel, a split, stained log, was placed more than seven feet above the hearth and only a foot below the ceiling. A variation to the box-like rooms was provided by placing the fireplaces in a corner of each of the two bedrooms on the first floor, and by the use of a patterned fabric in some of the bedrooms on the second floor. This material was stripped away or painted over much later. When solid colored drapes were on the casement windows and coverlets on the beds (William preferred red), and fur and Indian rugs placed on the floors, the overall effect was far more integrated and warmer than is evident today.

Besides the two bedrooms and baths on the first floor, the lodge had five bedrooms and two baths on the second floor and two bedrooms, two baths, a playroom and a store room on the third floor (the third floor rooms may have been remodeled as a nursery for young Gloria Baker and her nurse). William said that he had built Sagamore for his mother and himself, but the lodge far exceeded his personal needs and it is likely that he intended to sell Sagamore from the very start.

Near the chalet was the dining complex (Fig. 87) that combined the same basic components found at Uncas: a dining room, kitchen, laundry, enclosed drying yard, and an ice house and cooler. House staff had rooms above the kitchen. A screened-in porch off the dining room was used for meals in warm weather. These buildings were of frame construction, on stone basements, with sidings of spruce slabs and sheets of cedar bark set within square frames of split cedar poles.

The photograph of the dining room (Fig. 88) suggests what its counterpart at Uncas might have looked like, since their proportions were very much alike. The striped tablecloth and folding canvas chairs added exactly the right informality to what might otherwise have been the dining room of a club for men in the city. A window seat like those at Uncas is on one side of the room. Against the opposite wall is a sideboard with bottles of red wine and a metal teapot that gleams in the light of flames fueled by a gas generator in the basement.

On the lake to one side of the dining room complex was a dressing house and an open camp from which a wooden walk extended to a bathing dock. A covered "boat landing" was built on the opposite side of the point.

The farm buildings at Sagamore were more extensive than anything at Pine Knot or Uncas, and constituted a separate enclave, as shown in one of Stoddard's 1899 photographs (Fig. 89). These included a root cellar, blacksmith's shop, a cottage for "help" (later a school house for the Collins children), a wagon barn, a barn for horses, a guides' house (occupied by the electrician and his wife after 1915), a large wood shed and a "paint and carpenter's shop." There also were several other structures, such as a cow barn, chicken house and pig pen. Between these farm buildings and the lodge was a large garden for vegetables and flowers, enclosed by a high fence to keep out deer. Another garden, for corn and potatoes, was located on the opposite side of Sagamore Lake, together with a pasture and milking shed for cows in summer and a large shed for boiling maple sap into syrup in the spring.

106

One wonders what William had in mind for a farm seemingly capable of meeting the needs for far more people than occupied the camp before 1901. Perhaps he envisaged surpluses of food which might be sold to camps and hotels in the area. We will probably never know, for events were rapidly catching up with William at the time of Sagamore's completion in the spring of 1900, and he was forced to sell the property — 1,526 acres, buildings and furnishings — to Mr. and Mrs. Alfred G. Vanderbilt in June or July, 1901 for $162,500. William told Morgan that he had spent $140,000 in building Sagamore.

Vanderbilt, who had inherited $36.5 million while a junior at Yale College in 1898, added a number of buildings to Sagamore, notably the Amusement Hall and Lakeside, a guest cottage, in 1901, and a bowling alley between 1901 and 1914. The Amusement Hall is of considerable interest because it was designed by William L. Coulter, an architect who had moved to Saranac Lake about 1895 and quickly established a specialty, carried on by successive partners in his firm, of designing large camps in the Adirondacks for bankers, industrialists and other Americans of wealth. The connection between Durant and Coulter is unknown, but in 1902 William advised Mrs. Lucy Carnegie, widow of Andrew Carnegie's brother, that the Adirondack Hardware Company in Saranac Lake was doing work at Sagamore and that they had an architect designing new cottages for the Vanderbilts. That would seem to mean Coulter, given his signed design for the Amusement Hall (Fig. 92). Coulter is said to have acknowledged William West Durant's contribution to a woodland style of architecture, and a partner, William G. Distin (1884–1970), who carried the firm's reputation for camp design into the late 1940's, spoke of the pioneering role of the Durant camps on more than one occasion.

Sagamore was seldom visited between 1903 and 1911, according to a pamphlet by Howard Applegate. Divorced in 1908, Alfred married Margaret Emerson McKim in 1911, inaugurating thereafter a succession of building projects that continued after his death on the *Lusitania* in 1915. Electricity was installed that year and two large cottages, one for laundry and staff and the other, called the Wigwam, for guests, were erected. William's dining room was greatly enlarged in 1924 to accommodate seventy-five, a gun room replaced the summer dining porch and a wing was attached to the kitchen as a dining room for staff. Margaret's marriage of ten years to R. T. Baker, director of the U.S. Mint, ended in divorce in 1928, and she resumed her maiden name, Emerson. Each of her three children had a rustic cottage at Sagamore: George's was remodeled from the staff cottage near the kitchen, and Alfred's and Gloria's cottages were built by Thomas Callahan five or so years later, about 1935–37.

Up to World War II, Sagamore was a rendezvous for entertainers, statesmen and other public figures who willingly submitted to what Applegate said was Mrs. Emerson's tireless playing of indoor and outdoor games, gaining Sagamore the reputation as headquarters of the "gaming crowd." Mrs. Emerson, who served in the Pacific during the war with the American Red Cross, deeded Sagamore to Syracuse University about 1950, "to enable the expansion and diversification of continuing education programs." For nearly a quarter century the university operated Sagamore as a conference center. As previously noted, the university, hard pressed for money, sold Sagamore in 1975. The forest was cut by a jobber, and the bulk of the lands, including the farm enclave with its buildings, were sold for $550,000 to New York State. Many of the furnishings were auctioned at a public sale (Fig. 94). The lodge and adjoining buildings on about seven acres of land were conveyed in a state-approved restrictive deed through the Preservation League of New York, a private preservation organization, to the National Humanistic Education Center which continued to use Sagamore as a conference center, in which capacity it has functioned admirably, to the credit of its first builder, William West Durant.

Kamp Kill Kare

Despite the corny name given to it by Timothy and Cora (as in Lake Kora) Woodruff, Kamp Kill Kare was the most stylish and replete of the grand camps built in the Adirondacks. And so it remains to this day, thanks to its careful maintenance for more than sixty-five years by the Garvan family. William West Durant did not play a direct role in the design and construction of Kill Kare. He sold the 1,030 acre preserve for $12,360 to the Woodruffs in 1897. Included was a cabin, called Camp Omonsom, which had been built for him and Dr. Arpad Gerster some time prior to 1888. Durant never claimed credit for Kill Kare, though he readily advanced his authorship of camps elsewhere. The stone work and some of the furniture at Kill Kare before its destruction by fire in 1915 make it likely that some of the men who worked at Pine Knot and Uncas were employed by the Woodruffs. Too important to leave out of our story, Kill Kare is discussed here on the pretext of William's admittedly tenuous connections with it.

The earliest camp on Sumner Lake, renamed Kora by the Woodruffs, was Camp Omonsom, a snug log cabin built before 1888 for Durant and Arpad Gerster by Josh Smith and Jerry Little. By about 1893 a small kitchen and porch had been added (Fig. 95). Omonsom and later Fish Camp, a "box" built on Sneed Creek 3½ miles distant about 1893, were in country amply supplied with fish and deer yet easily accessible from camps and hotels on Raquette Lake to the north. Provisioned with food staples and firewood, and capable of accommodating parties of two to four, these camps away from camp were placed at the disposal of Governor Frank S. Black and other officials in a position to render help in Albany if it were needed.

Dr. Gerster, who never returned to his practice as a surgeon in New York City without contemplating his next trip to the Adirondacks, used Omonsom on many occasions. Once, with William's permission and just before closing up the camp, he fired his European rifle at a heavy boiler plate shutter and made a neat hole in it at seventy-five feet. Gerster watched with resignation as the terrain over which he had roamed with joyful abandon was systematically divided into smaller preserves and developed with roads, camps and farms, observing in his journal, ". . . the change 'for the better' is very saddening; but that was and is the natural course of events in all the beautiful, lovely places in the woods."

It was at supper at Camp Uncas on August 8, 1897 that William informed Dr. Gerster that the state had bought Township 6 at an "acceptable price" and that Woodruff had "bought for himself the Sumner Lake property, where I had fished and hunted these last ten years, thanks to the generosity of Mr. Durant." The surgeon, mindful that "This is, then, very likely the last season when I shall be permitted to enjoy the beauties of Sumner Lake," asked if William would sell him an island on Long Lake, to which Durant "cheerfully acceeded." A month later, when Gerster paid a call on Mrs. Woodruff, "a restless inquisitive body, with a perpetual choreatic twitch of her lip and left cheek," he discovered the changes that the Woodruffs had made in the brief perod they had been in possession of the camp:

> At the old camp we found Gov. Lounsbury [see Echo Camp above] sitting on the newly enlarged verandah, ornamented with artistic iron lamps and other city gimcracks. . . . the camp, which was originally built for me, was shown in its transformed shape. The shelf built for Johnnie's [his son, later a distinguished surgeon] bed by A. Fartin, had been taken down, the kitchen was made into a dining room, and part of the woodshed was converted into the kitchen. All the bushes sheltering the shore were cut away, exposing the camp to the lake.

Further alterations had been made by the time of his next visit, on August 13, 1898:

At the landing a boy met me, and took me into 'Killkare Camp' where Lieut. Gov. Woodruff received me, and took me into the bedroom, where Mrs. W., somewhat indisposed, lay in her bed in the darkened room by lamplight. They have built up and extended the old camp, and have done it evidently under the guidance of someone of good taste. A bathroom, hot & cold water, laundry, etc., etc., mark a wide departure from former conditions at Sumner. They have now a splendid camp. . . .

A new road, started the year before, provided easy access to Kill Kare from Sagamore Lodge.

The Gerster family moved their summer home to Long Lake shortly after the turn of the century, first residing in a camp on an island and then, in 1904–05, moving to a new camp, Kwenogamac, on the mainland nearby. Dr. Gerster and several members of the family are buried in the woods not far distant. Except for names carved into the surface of two giant boulders, there is no evidence of human intrusion.

By March, 1899 the Woodruff's camp had become a showplace, as indicated by James S. Whipple's description quoted at the beginning of this chapter. In February, 1903, Henry Wellington Wack, a lawyer turned travel and camping writer, wrote in *Field and Stream* magazine, of which he was the founder-editor, that, "Of the three [camps besides Uncas and Sagamore], Kamp Kill Kare is by far the most picturesque and mostly completely furnished — from birch-bark writing paper to the furniture made on the spot of cedar logs — which give the camp the rusticity and the atmosphere of the wilderness." Noting that the camp "has had many notable politicians and State officials in its cozy fold," Wack said that the Woodruffs had acquired a gondola from Italy the year before and that a cottage, called the "Kabin," built on an island on the lake for Mr. Woodruff, was a "symposium of sport," containing ". . . phonographs, ping-pong tables, an Aeolian piano, a library, a buffet stocked with every 'medicinal comfort' known to 'mixology' [cocktails?], all sorts of nooks and corners made bewilderingly interesting with mounted specimens of fur, fin and feather."

Gerster's remarks of his visits of 1897 and 1898 make it apparent that the log cottage called Omonsom was absorbed into the main building, which by about 1902 had achieved the appearance shown in **Figure 97**, and consisted of five attached or semi-attached buildings connected on the outside by a ground-level verandah largely covered by three roofs supported by rustic cedar columns. The ease with which these building units were integrated into a large structural composition and made to seem at home with the site, a knoll within easy viewing distance of the lake but set well back from it, contrasted with the more self-conscious architecture at Uncas and Sagamore. Kill Kare reintroduced the element of playfulness that charmed visitors to Pine Knot and left others, such as Whipple and Wack, preferring Kill Kare to Uncas and Sagamore.

An architect surely designed the main building, but we can only speculate who this might have been, possibly Grosvenor Atterbury or William L. Coulter, both previously mentioned in connection with Uncas and Sagamore. As for the furnishings or decor at Kill Kare, we have Dr. Gerster's critical observations: in 1897 he called them "city gimcracks," but by 1898 he qualified this by saying that the enlargement of Kill Kare had been done "evidently under the guidance of someone of good taste," a favorable recommendation indeed from a man not inclined to give easy praise.

Cora Woodruff and a Charles Hiscoe may have shared in the novel interior decoration of Kamp Kill Kare. Mrs. Woodruff, the daughter of the mayor of Poughkeepsie, was credited by Henry Wellington Wack when he wrote, in 1903, that "Mrs. Woodruff's provident hand has done the work of genius [at Kill Kare] with taste and forethought," a compliment which might be dismissed as a courtesy except for an article in the *Brooklyn Eagle* for May 27, 1900 which said that she had been responsible for the "artistic remodeling" of the Woodruffs' residence in Brooklyn.

Captain Hiscoe, formerly an officer in the British army, assisted the Woodruffs in designing and furnishing the Kabin which was built on an island on Lake Kora in 1901. According to Anthony N. B. Garvan, Hiscoe returned to Kill Kare in 1909 and he supervised the rebuilding and furnishing of the camp for Mr. and Mrs. Garvan, very much along the old lines, following the fire which destroyed the entire main building in 1915 (Fig. 98). Dr. Garvan, a historian and son of the Garvans, likened Hiscoe to a "chief clerk of the works," a title used to describe men who planned and supervised construction projects in Europe and America before the advent of the professional architect and engineer in the nineteenth century.

The city park movement of the 1850's and after was another possible source of influence on Kill Kare and the other camps of the Adirondacks. Woodruff, who had a considerable income from several businesses, was Park Commissioner for the City of Brooklyn for a brief period before being elected in 1896 to the first of three terms as Lieutenant Governor. At Brooklyn's Prospect Park and particularly at Central Park in New York City there was a steady development, after the Civil War, of walks, paths, and artificial lakes and streams carefully planned to provide city dwellers with a respite from the pressures of city life. Enhancing the outdoor qualities of these parks were a variety of what an eighteenth century writer called "factitious accompaniments," that is, shelters, pergolas, benches, bridges and so on, which were often built of rustic materials, principally cedar, and were considered indispensable components of the modern urban park. Venitian gondolas were introduced to Central Park before 1869, and they were still being used, along with a variety of other exotic boats, at the turn of the century, when the Woodruffs placed the gondola *Venice* on Lake Kora in the Adirondacks.

Newspapers in the city and the Adirondack region carried the names of hundreds of families coming to the Adirondacks for the summer season. (See, for example, the *New York Tribune* for August 24, 1902.) Many among this perennial invasion, perhaps starting in the 1890's, had been introduced to the outdoors and recreation principally through city parks like those in New York City and Brooklyn. William West Durant was born in Brooklyn and, like Timothy Woodruff, his family had a home there. As noted above, his father sold a large tract of land to the city in 1869 for an extension of Prospect Park. The evidence is tenuous and circumstantial, but an argument might be made for showing that rustic construction in the Adirondacks was influenced as much by the city as by skills and materials native to the Adirondacks. The carrying of this seed to the wilds can be found, perhaps, in an idea in the poem, "The Adirondacs," written by Ralph Waldo Emerson following his camping trip in 1858 to Follensby Pond with other luminaries from Boston and Cambridge: "We flee from cities, but we bring/The best of cities with us. . . ." Another area in need of further study are European sources of influence on rustic design in the U.S.

Cora Woodruff died in 1904 and her husband married again the following year. Shortly before his death in October, 1913, Kill Kare was deeded to Alfred G. Vanderbilt who conveyed it to Mr. and Mrs. Francis P. Garvan on December 11, 1914. The Garvans, who had been introduced to the Adirondacks by Robert J. Collier, had scarcely occupied the camp when it was destroyed by fire in 1915. Some of the furnishings were salvaged and were put in its replacement, a structure similar in construction and spirit, if not in detail

(Fig. 99). This work and the camp's extensive enlargement was undertaken by one of the foremost architects of the day, John Russell Pope, designer of an addition to the Metropolitan Museum of Art in New York and the National Gallery of Art in Washington.

By 1930, according to an insurance report, Kamp Kill Kare encompassed thirty buildings or structures:

> The Main Camp consisting of four attached buildings: 1) dining room, laundry and servant's quarters, 2) children's building and library, 3) The Casino, a living room; and 4) Mrs. Garvan's "living room cabin" containing locally made rustic furniture, including a bedstead formed by a full-size tree (Fig. 100).
>
> A large boathouse-and-residence for Mr. Garvan, a two-story structure containing a large living room, library and several private bedrooms on the second floor.
>
> The Kabin on the island, built for the Woodruffs about 1901 and accommodating about ten guests.
>
> Two rustic cottages, two stories and similar, one reserved for the superintendent and his assistants.
>
> A "playhouse, bowling alley, squash court and gun house," containing an early American taproom and collections of pewter and antique furniture on the first floor and, on the second, "fire arms, swords, pikes, powder horns numbering over 2,000 specimens" in all.
>
> A reproduction of a Norman chapel located in a clearing in the woods.
>
> Three cottages for the electrician and other resident employees, the largest containing a kitchen, big dining room, laundry and a pump room that was Kill Kare's original source of water before the construction of reservoirs.
>
> An eight-unit structure of massive stone construction consisting of dairy, cow barn, tower, carriage room, stables, wagon room, shops for the carpenter and blacksmith, and a playroom.
>
> "Kamp Keen Kut," formerly a cottage for men but "now used as a dance hall."
>
> A greenhouse and a gardner's cottage.
>
> Two ice houses, a cooler and dairy.
>
> A large woodshed about 100 feet long and 30 feet wide, open all around and containing about five hundred cords of firewood.
>
> Two lean-to's partly filled with balsam boughs.
>
> A small woodshed with hot water heater for the Kabin.
>
> A generator house and light plant.
>
> A pump house for the sewerage system.
>
> A pump house for water.
>
> Small boat house open on four sides for storage of row boats and canoes.
>
> Plus, silo, two farm buildings, hog house, tool house, storage building for dynamite and chemicals, a fish hatchery [removed by 1930] and spring house.

The principal buildings were heated by steam from basement boilers fueled by coal or wood.

Despite its elaboration in the hands of the Garvans, the part of Kill Kare with buildings was only about twenty acres. The thousand acres of forest around the camp were untouched except for the clearing of fallen timber and brush in the winter to reduce the hazard of fire. Much of the construction at Kill Kare was frame with spruce slab siding and wood shingles outside and open beam and rafter with board paneling inside. Clearly the most imposing buildings at Kill Kare and very likely in the entire Adirondacks were those

111

designed by Pope using native stones placed one on the other seemingly without the use of mortar (Fig. 101). Appropriately said to be a "Cyclopean" style of ashlar construction, the buildings are well proportioned despite their massive, squat construction and seem quite at home in their Adirondack surroundings.

Kamp Kill Kare embodied a life style of contradictions, in which simplicity existed side by side with luxury. Mr. and Mrs. Garvan's private railroad car could be found with a few others like it on the siding at Raquette Lake, and expansive gestures, such as bringing a chef from a restaurant like Delmonico's to prepare freshly caught trout, were not uncommon. Dr. Garvan, who inherited Kill Kare with other members of the family following his mother's death in 1978, concludes that his parents did such things "because they were the difficult thing to do." They protected the woods, he says, and took care in laying out trails and keeping evidence of human presence to a minimum. As a result, the property, except for the small proportion set aside for the camp itself, is very much as it was when it was sold by William West Durant in 1897. Blue noses among the lovers of the outdoors find comforts like those afforded by Kill Kare in earlier years to be an indulgence in which the discomforts and hazards of the wilds were carefully deleted. Nature entertains many kinds of foolishness, not the least of which may be the hiker attempting slumber in a wet sleeping bag. The grand camps fostered a style of living fondly recalled by those who experienced it. Relaxation, conviviality and privacy were probably more important to the large camps than ostentation. People showed off in the presence of strangers, at hotels or clubs. The large Adirondack camps were too isolated to encourage much wandering. To a large degree, they were self-contained, offering all the necessities and pleasures of life in their own spacious back yards.

Camp Uncas

Fig. 75   The Manor House at Camp Uncas was built by William West Durant in 1893–94, probably with the assistance of a professional architect. Sold to J. Pierpont Morgan in 1896, the year it was photographed by R. T. Stratton, the property combined a large preserve with cottages, service buildings, a farm and roads, all components of the Camp Beautiful in the Adirondacks. Adirondack Museum.

Fig. 76   *The living room of the manor House at Camp Uncas, showing the ceiling beams of logs and window seats adopted shortly after at Sagamore Lodge and Kamp Kill Kare. The fireplace abutted the fireplace in Fig. 78. Photograph by R. T. Stratton, 1896. Adirondack Museum.*

Fig. 77   This watercolor design for a cabinet and desk at Camp Uncas bears the signature "Grosvenor Atter-
bury" over which "W. W. Durant" has been inscribed, with the date "June, 1893." A visitor at Camp Pine Knot,
Atterbury was a young architect who may have assisted Durant in designing the Manor House. Adirondack
Museum, gift of Mrs. Bromley Seeley.

Fig. 78   The master bedroom of the Manor House at Camp Uncas, showing the post and beam construction,
window seat and cantilevered mantel over the fireplace. The photograph, taken in the 1960's, reveals that Uncas
looked much as it had in Durant's and Morgan's time. Photograph by James Fynmore, Adirondack Museum.

Fig. 79   *The dining hall at Camp Uncas, located a minute's walk from the Manor House, may have resembled the dining room built at Sagamore several years later (Fig. 88). William introduced stone basements and furnaces at Uncas. Mohegan Lake appears in this photograph of 1896 by R. T. Stratton. Adirondack Museum.*

Fig. 80   *Chingachgook, one of two log cottages at Camp Uncas, in a photograph of the 1960's. The buildings at Camp Uncas deteriorated and many original furnishings were dispersed after the property became a camp for Boy Scouts in the sixties. Photograph by James Fynmore, Adirondack Museum.*

Fig. 81 Anne Morgan rebuilt Durant's dining hall, enlarging it with the addition of upstairs rooms and a twenty foot fireplace. The quality of Durant's stonework is apparent in a comparison of his chimney, to the right, with its larger neighbor of a decade or so later. Author's photograph.

Fig. 82 The dining room at Camp Uncas as remodeled by Anne Morgan. The ironwork at Uncas – hinges, latches, lamps, fireplace equipment and chandeliers – was fashioned by a blacksmith at Uncas. A low bench enabled people to sit close by the fire. Photograph by James Fynmore, Adirondack Museum.

Sagamore Lodge

Fig. 83 William West Durant's other camps melted into the woods, but Sagamore Lodge, built in 1897 from his designs, stood prominently on a landscaped clearing. Needing money, he sold the property in 1901 to Alfred G. Vanderbilt, who had inherited a large fortune a few years before. Vanderbilt is seated far right, his favorite dog Stormy stands left, in a photograph of 1912–15. Richard Collins, the superintendent, holds a horse from the side. The silver cup on the porch was awarded the man who stayed longest on a toboggan during a three-day "crack the whip" contest on Sagamore Lake. Adirondack Museum.

Fig. 84   The "Sitting Room" of Sagamore Lodge, from an album of photographs made specially for Durant by Seneca Ray Stoddard in 1899. Durant's portrait (see Fig. 8) is on the table next to a model of a Swiss chalet. Adirondack Museum.

Fig. 85 "East Bedroom, 2nd Story," Sagamore Lodge, 1899. Durant experimented with his designs for fireplaces at Sagamore. This one elevated the mantel about eighteen inches from the ceiling and had an irregularly shaped panel below of textured red clay. Adirondack Museum.

Fig. 86   "East Bedroom," first floor, Sagamore Lodge, 1899. This was William's room, to judge by the desk, pictures and leather bag. The fireplace occupied the corner of the room. Adirondack Museum.

Fig. 87   The dining room complex at Sagamore Lodge combined, from left to right, a screened-in dining porch, dining room (Fig. 88), kitchen and staff dining room, laundry, ice house and cooler, and a drying yard. Bedrooms for women on the staff were above the kitchen area. The photograph was taken by Stoddard in 1899. Adirondack Museum.

Fig. 88 *The dining room at Sagamore Lodge, 1899. The trophies on the wall may have been bagged by Durant. His dual tie to the U.S. and England is revealed by the flags at the window. Gas provided illumination in the principal rooms at Sagamore at this time. Adirondack Museum.*

Fig. 89 *The farm buildings at Sagamore Lodge, 1899. The root cellar and blacksmith's shop are nearest the camera. New York State acquired this enclave when it purchased the preserve (exclusive of the chalet and its nearby buildings) for $550,000 in 1975. Adirondack Museum.*

Fig. 90   This aerial view of Sagamore Lodge shows the main complex as built by Durant and expanded by Vanderbilt and his widow, Margaret Emerson. The Amusement Hall, built in 1901, is to the left. Behind it is a two-lane bowling alley. Today the camp is owned by the National Humanistic Education Center, which operates it as a conference facility. Photograph by Peter and Rosine Lemon, Adirondack Museum.

Fig. 91   Ground plan of Sagamore Lodge and its farms, based on plans of 1898 and 1 by William West Durant. Excluded are additions after 1900. Sagamore produced much of own food – milk, eggs, meat and vegetables. In addition it had a greenhouse in which se lings were started for flower beds and window boxes. Drawn by Richard Youngken, Adir dack Museum.

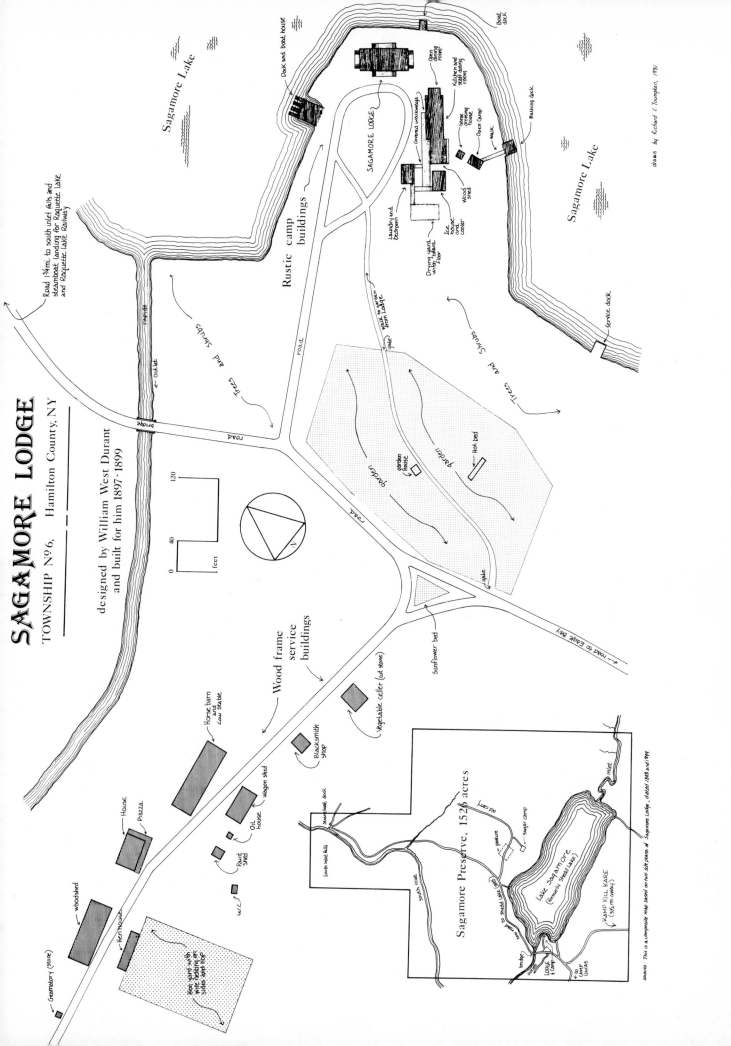

Sagamore Lodge

TOWNSHIP No 6, Hamilton County, NY

designed by William West Durant and built for him 1897 - 1899

drawn by Richard C. Youngken, 1981

Sagamore Lake

Sagamore Lake

Sagamore Lake

Dock and boat house

Boat dock

Open dining room

Kitchen and staff dining room

Game dressing house

Bathing dock

Open Camp

Covered walkways

Walk

SAGAMORE LODGE

Rustic camp buildings

Wood shed

Laundry and bathroom

Ice house and cooler

Drying yard with island floor

Walk to garden from Lodge

gate

Service dock

Trees and Shrubs

garden

garden house

garden

Hot bed

gate

road

Rapids

← outlet

Road 1¾ mi. to south inlet falls and steamboat landing for Raquette Lake and Raquette Lake Railway

Trees and shrubs

bridge

road

road

N

0   40   120
feet

Sunflower bed

← road to Eagle Bay

Wood frame service buildings

Vegetable cellar (cut stone)

Blacksmith shop

Wagon Shed

Oil house

Paint Shed

Horse barn and Cow Stable

w.c.

House

Piazza

Woodshed

Hen house

Creamatory (stone)

Hen yard with wire fencing on sides and top

Sagamore Preserve, 1526 acres

Steamboat dock

South Inlet falls

south inlet

to Shed Lake

to Inlet Camp

old road

pasture

Sugar Camp

inlet

Lake Sagamore (formerly Shed Lake)

KAMP KILL KARE (3½ mi. away)

bridge

outlet

LODGE & Camp

to CAMP UNCAS

SOURCE : This is a composite map based on two site plans of Sagamore Lodge, dated 1898 and 1899.

Fig. 92   Detail of the design for the Amusement Hall at Sagamore Lodge, signed by William L. Coulter and dated 1901. Durant sold Sagamore the year Coulter made this design for its new owners, Mr. and Mrs. Vanderbilt. A professional architect who settled in Saranac Lake for his health, Coulter, with the firm's later partners, designed large Adirondack camps whose variety, amenities and detailing had been explored a generation earlier by William West Durant. Drawing courtesy of Wareham-DeLair Architects, Saranac Lake, N.Y.

Fig. 93   A bathroom at Sagamore Lodge, 1899. Sagamore's success lay not just in what could be seen, but in the water, sanitary, heating and gas generating systems which were out of sight but offered city comforts in the heart of the Adirondack wilds. Adirondack Museum.

Fig. 94   Auction at Sagamore Lodge, October 10, 1976. Mrs. Emerson gave the Sagamore property to Syracuse University about 1950. After years of operating it as a conference center, the University, hard pressed for cash, sold the timber to a jobber, the land to New York State and some of the furnishings to bidders at this public auction. Author's photograph.

Kamp Kill Kare

Fig. 95   Camp Omonsom was built in the eighties on Sumner Lake as a hunting and fishing retreat for Durant and Dr. Arpad Gerster, and their friends. The small cabin was incorporated into the complex erected on the site in 1897–99 by Lt. Gov. and Mrs. Timothy Woodruff (Fig. 97), who renamed the camp and its lake, Camp Kill Kare and Lake Kora. William's wife Janet is said to be on the porch in a photograph of c. 1892. Adirondack Museum.

Fig. 96   A "Guest Chamber" at Kamp Kill Kare, c. 1900–05. By 1900 Kill Kare had become the most pictur-esque of the large camps in the region. Rooms, such as this, done in "wood brown," were carefully decorated, perhaps by Mrs. Woodruff with the aid of Capt. Charles Hiscoe, formerly a British officer. Adirondack Museum, courtesy of Mrs. Francis P. Garvan.

Fig. 97   *Kamp Kill Kare, Lake Kora, c. 1900. The principal buildings at Kill Kare were perfectly integrated on a slope that dropped gently to the lake. The verandah, sheltered by several roofs, and level with the ground, provided a natural transition between the outdoors and interior rooms. Adirondack Museum.*

Fig. 98   *The Woodruff estate sold Kamp Kill Kare to Alfred G. Vanderbilt in 1913, and he conveyed it a year later to Mr. and Mrs. Francis P. Garvan. In 1915 the principal complex burned to the ground, as seen in a photograph of the smouldering ruins taken the next day. Photograph courtesy of the John C. Collins Family.*

Fig. 100 One of the most extraordinary examples of rustic construction is Mrs. Garvan's bed, with one post formed by a tree with an owl perched in its branches and a footboard serving as backrest of a rustic bench. Much of the furniture at Kill Kare was made locally. Capt. Hiscoe returned to assist the Garvans with the redecoration of the camp following the 1915 fire. Photograph by Richard Linke (1974), Adirondack Museum.

Fig. 99 *Kamp Kill Kare, Lake Kora, c. 1917. The Garvans rebuilt the main camp very much along the same exterior lines as its predecessor. Mrs. Garvan's cottage, left, with a bed fashioned from a tree (Fig. 100), was added, together with the boathouse and residence shown under construction in this panoramic photograph by H. M. Beach. Adirondack Museum.*

Fig. 101 *Much of the expansion of Kamp Kill Kare, including an eight unit series of stone buildings for a dairy, cow barn, stable, carriage room, etc., was under the supervision of John Russell Pope, a leading architect of the period. The mode of construction, called "Cyclopean" because of the large stones employed, was without precedent in the Adirondacks. Adirondack Museum.*

The Trial   10

William West Durant and his lawyers delayed going to trial for nearly five years following his sister's first legal action against him. The trial began on January 5, 1899 in New York
City and continued for six or seven days. Friends, witnesses and lawyers for both sides
assembled in the courtroom, together with spectators and reporters whose accounts were
followed by readers in the next day's newspapers. The purpose of the trial, which was not
held before a jury, was to determine whether William should be required to submit an
accounting of Dr. Thomas Clark Durant's estate during those years William administered it
for his mother, his sister and himself.

Heloise Durant Rose was represented by John E. Parsons and Lucius N. Palmer of the
firm of Parsons, Shepard and Ogden at 111 Broadway. This was the ninth legal firm engaged by Ella since 1886. William's attorney was Freling H. Smith of the law firm of Smith
and Simpson at 115 Broadway, but his counsels at the trial were Harry W. Simpson and
Carlisle Norwood. Smith and Simpson had been associates of William's in other matters,
dating back to 1889 when the Adirondack Railroad was sold to the Delaware and Hudson
Canal Company. Smith's signature appears as an entry in the guest book at Camp Pine
Knot dated August 10, 1893, and he was once paid more than $17,000 for other legal
services to Durant. Presiding at the trial was Judge Miles Beach, a justice of the State
Supreme Court. The testimony and exhibits, mostly letters, were printed in 1903 as a
record for appeal to the Appellate Division of the Supreme Court.

Ella contended that her brother had told her in 1885 that their father's estate was
worth $1.5 million and that it would be equally divided between their mother and them. It
was with this understanding that she signed over power of attorney to him; not, however,
without having first been importuned by her mother and John L. Barbour, a lawyer and
friend of the family. William, she testified, had said that he and his mother could freeze her
out if she refused to cooperate. The confrontation took place in Mrs. Durant's bedroom,
possibly while the doctor's body lay in the drawing room downstairs. Ella was called up
from the drawing room. Somebody closed the door behind her, she said, as she moved to
the foot of her mother's bed. William started the conversation:

"A. He said that we being two women and he being the man of the family, that it was
naturally right he should attend to our affairs . . . and he had mother's power of
attorney and he wanted mine . . . , and then when the [rail]road was sold and the land
[too], that there would be some debts to be paid, and after that there would be about a
million and a half [dollars] coming to us. . . .

Q. I [Ella's attorney] understood you to say that at first you hesitated. . . .
A. Yes . . . because I had not seen it [the document] then; my mother turned around
to Mr. Barbour and Mr. Hall* and said, 'Well, if my daughter objects, I didn't, because I signed one,' and she said she had entire confidence in my brother. I said it was

*Amos Hall bought land for the Durants. He may have been a relative on the doctor's side of the family.

132

not a question of confidence, that he always told me never to sign a paper until I read it.

Q. Was anything said by your brother upon the subject of what would occur if you did not sign this power of attorney?

A. Yes, he had said that we were all in the same boat . . . that of course we being three having equal interests, that two could freeze-out the other one. I [said I] did not quite understand the expression. . . . My brother said, turning to Mr. Barbour, 'That is American law, too, isn't it,' and [Barbour] said yes. I was not at the time experienced in business matters. I had been writing — writing poetry and books, devoting myself to literary pursuits and mission work."

She testified that her brother had never given her an accounting of the estate, and that he and Barbour had made false representations that the estate was swamped by claims against it. At about the time William wrote her in England to say that the Adirondack Railway Company's bonds and stocks were nearly valueless, he was offering, on May 25, 1886, to sell Dr. Durant's estate to Daniel Odell for more than $1.3 million. Barbour's assertion to her on April 14, 1887 that there was a $20 million judgment against the estate, was likewise untrue or misleading. Dr. Durant had obtained a release from it long before and, she said, "this judgment that was pending was spoken of in the family as a joke." In recent years, her brother had been selling some of the lands originally belonging to the estate or transferring titles to some tracts from himself to other persons.

The trial was a personal tragedy for the family. The culmination of long-standing grudges and habits dating back many years, it was also a drama of high order, a fitting last act to the Victorian era, when men ruled their homes and businesses yet found their control increasingly challenged by women and subordinates no longer willing to accept subjugation as the price for genteel poverty.

Ella must have been the center of attention in the courtroom. Dark and beautiful, slender like her brother, she was a solitary figure. Unlike her brother, who literally had family and associates sitting on his side in the courtroom (as her lawyer stated), she had but three to testify for her — two associates of her father's and Frances Murphy, a friend who recalled William's complaints about his father during the summer of 1883. She was her own chief witness, and her responses to questions from William's attorney, who attempted to insinuate that her past life of artistic figures and poor business investments somehow had a bearing on the merits of her complaint against her brother, were poised and coherent, at least as they appeared in the printed record. A newspaper account, however, said that Ella "visibly showed emotion" during questioning about her father's anger with her in 1881.

William's defense, more elaborate than his sister's complaint, followed from the premise that their father Dr. Durant was in debt to his wife in 1885. The indebtedness dated back to 1847 when Hannah Timbrell Durant turned several thousand dollars over to him shortly after their marriage. That money, together with what she received on occasion from Dr. Durant, was later used to purchase a tract of land which was condemned by the city of Brooklyn on February 24, 1869 for what became a part of Prospect Park. Mrs. Durant was awarded $236,382 for the land, a princely sum in those days, and the money was borrowed by her husband, her legal agent, who put it in his account and invested it in Adirondack properties, including a lumber mill in North Creek.

Between October 6, 1871 and March 11, 1872, Dr. Durant assigned securities to his wife in exchange for cash; the securities carried face values in excess of the amounts borrowed in cash. The assignment of certificates of stocks and bonds presumably reflected Dr.

Durant's debt to his wife. According to William, she received securities valued at $823,765 out of a total worth $1,166,199. He and his sister were assigned far smaller shares, $48,672 apiece. Because the Delaware and Hudson purchased the certificates at half their face value, he and Ella each received $24,336.

Mr. Parsons, Ella's counsel, raised the question, however, whether all the certificates had indeed been signed over to Dr. Durant's widow. Many records were missing, and the books of the Adirondack Railway Company appeared to have "interlineations" of a date subsequent to the original entries, perhaps inserted by John T. Banker, an aged book-keeper with years of service to the Durant family. William Sutphen, who was Dr. Durant's "confidential advisor" and a co-trustee with William for the estate, testified that he knew that the certificates were issued to Mrs. Durant because Dr. Durant had told him so during frequent conferences with the doctor at his New York City office.

The thrust of William's defense was given in a later summation to his appeal. Dr. Durant was "not restrained by settling a preference on his wife" at the expense of others. She was, after all, his "heaviest creditor." At this, William's lawyers turned the judge's attention to Ella. She was, they said, the "storm center of family discord," she "could not keep money" and was "violent, unruly and disobedient." Her confirmation into the Epis-copal Church took place at an "institution for the redemption of abandoned women." [But this may have been missionary work.] Little wonder, they concluded, that Dr. Durant was not more generous with his daughter: "Is it at all odd that these traits of character were distasteful and served to alienate her from the other members of the family?" On the other hand, they added, "Whatever was saved from the family ruin was saved by the defendant."

William, however, had received no more from his father than his sister. How did he acquire his fortune? William contended that he had amassed the fortune on his own and that most of the estate had come to his mother, for whom he served as legal agent. Gener-ally the court did not go along with these claims, for reasons never explicitly stated in the record of testimony examined. Heloise's assertion, that William had put the estate's lands into the names of other parties, who transferred them to the Forest Park & Land Com-pany, was a fair description and seems to have been upheld. The documents which John Barbour brought to North Creek on the day of Dr. Durant's death were significantly differ-ent, though Ella was certainly not aware of it at the time. The doctor's widow signed a paper granting full legal power in *all* of her affairs to William, while the one signed by Ella limited William's responsibility only to that portion of the estate specifically assigned to her. When he turned over $24,336 to his sister in London in 1899, following the sale of the Adirondack Railway Company, his fiduciary obligations to her were terminated, according to its terms.

William's acquisition of lands in the Adirondacks was achieved largely through that sale. The trial brought out the broader strategy by which that had been accomplished. Prior to the sale, a large portion of lands embodied in the stocks and bonds of the company were "stripped" from the certificates. About 370,000 of 450,000 acres was separated from the Adirondack Railway Company's holdings and deeded to Robert W. Cromley, who then conveyed them to William West Durant. The remainder, about 80,000 acres, was presum-ably included in the sale to the Delaware and Hudson.

Cromley was a clerk in the law office of William's attorney, Freling Smith. In examin-ing William during the 1899 trial, Ella's counsel, John E. Parsons, inquired about this roundabout transaction:

"Q. Was there any legal reason why the Adirondack Railway Company, if it desired to make you the owner of these lands should not make a deed directly to you?

A. None whatever. . . . I think it was done.

Q. Don't you remember that the title to the property conveyed by this deed to Cromley never did get into your name; that there were other conduits as well as Cromley?

A. I don't at this moment."

William contended that the D&H had not wanted most of the railway company's lands and that he therefore purchased them for a consideration through Cromley and possibly the Adirondack Timber and Mineral Company. William gave the "consideration" to Cromley, who then conveyed the deed to William:

"Q. Did Cromley pay the $145,000?

A. It was paid, yes.

Q. Who did pay it?

A. I was the means of it being paid. I told you he was the conduit.

Q. Did you pay it?

A. I caused it to be paid."

There was no proof that the $145,000 "consideration" meant the exchange of cash:

"Q. There was no $145,000 in money, was there?

A. I think there was, or its equivalent."

William had been an apt pupil at his father's elbow. His negotiations in 1885–1889 resulted in the sale of the railroad, which was in debt and poor repair, and the retention of about four-fifths of the company's lands, some of which he sold. A hint that this was a long-range scheme came out when Ella's lawyer questioned William about the severing of lands from the company's certificates:

"Q. That was part of your trade, you were to get these lands?

A. It was part of the business that the land should come to me.

Q. So that whatever else you got on top of the mortages, you got the lands?

A. Yes. . . ."

In looking at the wealth that William amassed, it was difficult to separate earnings made on his own from those derived from the estate. An instance was the transactions in 1887–1888 when he acquired part of Township 5 and all of Townships 6 and 34. Ella's attorney asked William whether the Camp Uncas lands in Township 5 had belonged to the old Adirondack Company, to which William replied, "I don't think so . . . or a very small portion of them."

William West Durant had put himself in an untenable position. His closest friends could not have helped but wonder why he had allowed the family's intimate affairs to be dragged for a second time (following his suit for divorce) into the open at a public trial. He had been granted full responsibility and initiative in managing the estate left by his father, in accordance with the custom of concentrating authority on a single member of the family. This privilege conferred a correspondingly greater obligation on him to protect the interests of those dependent upon him. Abram Hewitt's stern rebuke in 1892, in which he told William that his sister's "eccentricities would not in any way change the obligation which I should feel to place her in an independent position," expressed this rule of domestic order and justice which William was seen to have violated.

Judge Miles Beach decided in Heloise Durant Rose's favor on January 24, 1899, about ten days after the conclusion of the trial. On February 23 he ruled that she was entitled to an accounting and one-third of the estate plus interest and costs. The deposit of the $30,000 option from Edward Crane to William's account justified, in the opinion of the judge, the rendering of an accounting. He appointed a referree, Augustus C. Brown, to receive the accounting from the defendant, make it available to the plaintiff for examination and to submit a report on which a final judgment might be reached.

William did not file a report until December 22, 1899, ten months after Judge Beach's decision. It was found to be "inadequate" the next month because it covered only that portion of Ella's inheritance as had passed through her brother's hands. On January 25 he was ordered to make a complete accounting within five days. He did not meet the deadline, for the following spring he was corresponding with one of his lawyers in an effort to locate the records which would satisfy the court.

Twenty months later, on October 8, 1901, he was ordered into court. The following December he was held in contempt and an order for his arrest was issued. Ten days later he was granted a stay pending his appeal to the Appellate Division. A newspaper account reported that he narrowly escaped arrest by giving the value of Dr. Durant's estate to the court-appointed referree.

The referree handed down his judgment on December 21, 1901: William owed his sister $753,931, of which $428,088 was her share and the remainder was interest. The award was affirmed by the court on January 11, the conclusion being that the power of attorney which Ella signed over to her brother covered the entire estate, since that was how it had been represented to her at the time of her father's death.

Ella would learn that she had won a Pyrrhic victory. She was still trying to get her brother into court in February, 1903 for a determination of his assets. His lawyer said he was residing at his "Adirondack estate" and that he preferred to serve a six month jail term in Hamilton County rather than New York City as an alternative to his inability to post $1.5 million in bond. He was safe in the Adirondacks since the sentence could be carried out only if he returned to the jurisdiction in which it was imposed.

William appealed the 1899 decision and lost. Judge Hatch summarized the case in ringing phrases that must have dogged William during the three decades left to him. The justice, quoted in the July 9, 1903 issue of *The New York Times*, said:

"This property came into the hands of the defendant as the trustee for the mother and sister. He evidently applied to its management business skill and judgement, and he produced, as doubtless Dr. Durant would have done had he lived, for these interests, a very large property; and by adroit manipulation, under power of attorney given by his mother and sister, without cost to himself in money outside what the property produced, he succeeded in vesting the title of the whole of this very large estate in himself. His mother became dependent, his sister languished in want, and he reveled in luxury."

Ella's attorney for the appeal was Charles Stewart Davison. How she managed to pay for legal services is not known, for at the time she described herself as "destitute."

Mossy Camp and
Other Newcomb Projects

11

In 1898 William extended his operations outside the Raquette Lake region for the first time since the sale of the railroad in 1889. He started construction of what he called Mossy Camp on Arbutus Lake, about 2½ miles west of the village of Newcomb and forty miles northeast of Raquette Lake. He divided his lands in this fresh territory into three preserves: the Arbutus Lake Preserve, consisting of the camp, farm and 1,536 acres of land, which he sold in 1900 to Collis P. Huntington's adopted stepson, Archer, for between fifty and sixty thousand dollars; the Zack Lake Preserve, a tract of about sixteen hundred acres; and the Goodenow Mountain Preserve, variously amounting to 478 or 1,000 acres (according to two maps), on the summit of which he built a hunting and fishing camp overlooking Zack Lake to the south and Rich Lake on the north. In addition he divided the north shore of Rich Lake into forty-two lots of three to seven acres each.

In a letter of December 21, 1899 to Archer, who had already seen Mossy Camp, William offered to sell either the Zack or Arbutus preserves, recommending the latter since "The camp is furnished and is now in magnificent order; its house and cooler is built to last, and with the finest log workmanship I have ever seen; and you are only a short distance from the Caughnawaga Club on one side and Mr. Pruyn of Albany on the other, and if I am to have a camp of my own on either Rich Lake or the [Goodenow] Mountain, why I would be a neighbor also." The negotiation for the sale was also conducted with Collis P. Huntington. After the transaction was completed in the spring of 1900, William wrote the highway commissioners asking that portions of the road to Newcomb from Long Lake be repaired in time for the new owner's arrival at the camp that summer.

The isolation of his Newcomb properties, together with his frantic efforts to manage his other projects in addition to his sister's lawsuit, made it necessary for William to rely on the abilities of the men working for him in Newcomb. Maurice Callahan, formerly telegraph operator at Camp Pine Knot, was the superintendent at Mossy Camp between 1898 and 1900. John Anderson, Jr., of North Creek, who seems to have been a foreman, directed men like Garry Rogers, Josh Smith, James B. Rexford, Charles Dougherty and Seth Alden, all from North Creek and North River, who did carpentry and masonry work (Alden) at Arbutus in 1898 and 1899. Principal contractor and supplier, W. J. Hammond, was an "agent builder" in Saratoga Springs. We do not know who designed the buildings at Mossy Camp, but at one point R. Newton Brezee, an architect in Saratoga Springs, was preparing plans for cottages at Zack Lake, either of his own design or from sketches sent by Durant.

Mossy Camp was built during the period that Sagamore was being constructed. It was smaller and far less prepossessing, which seems to have suited the young Mr. and Mrs. Huntington just fine. The appearance of the camp, however, cannot be easily reconstructed, for it was sold before Seneca Ray Stoddard had the opportunity to photograph it as William intended. The buildings subsequently underwent alterations that leave them with few distinguishing marks of their character in 1900. The camp consisted of a 1½ story cottage with siding of evenly cut boards imitating log slabs, with the bark removed and stained dark brown. This building contained a dining room in front, facing Arbutus Lake, and a kitchen in back. Attached on one side was a cottage for servants and at the rear were woodshed and ice house reached from the kitchen by a covered and enclosed walk. Fifty feet back and to one side of the main cottage was the "Owner's Cottage," a 1½ story structure of ample size, fifty by thirty-two feet. A boardwalk connected this cottage with a "Sleeping Cottage," and on the shore of the lake was a "Bachelor Cottage" together with a boathouse. The farm or service buildings were located about a quarter of a mile distant and consisted of a "Keeper's Cottage," a woodshed, store house and barn.

A feature at Mossy Camp was the stone work which utilized smooth round stones like those found in a lake, stream or gravel pit. The result was quite different from the quarried stone which William had used at Camp Pine Knot and Camp Uncas, and it was far less satisfying. William was dismayed when he made a detour to Newcomb on his way back from New York City. Writing Hammond on October 21, 1899, he said, ". . . the masons you sent were either incompetent men or else deliberately did poor work and wasted time. I have seen their work at Newcomb and am expecting to see in a few days the work they have done for me at Sagamore. I unhesitatingly say that in my opinion the work is poor at Arbutus and I have every reason to believe it equally so at Sagamore." A month later he wrote the contractor to say that Hammond's men "have done me harm" and that he would deduct twenty-five percent from the bill. Rubble stone work required less effort and artistry than the uncoursed and sensitively reticulated ashlar work at William's earlier camps. It also was a dreadful dust-catcher. The decline in quality was due to lack of supervision by William, but the pressure on him to build camps and sell them as rapidly as possible at this time must also have been a factor.

William constructed a fish hatchery below the outlet of Arbutus Lake and just behind a dam. A sluice-way diverted the necessary oxygen-rich flow of water through an elbow shaped concrete basin where the fish were placed until ready for the lake. The difficulty was getting the brook trout to Newcomb from the hatchery in Caledonia, a town south of Rochester and perhaps 150 miles by rail from North Creek. Five thousand trout were ordered in the spring of 1900, but the teamster who brought them on the last leg of their long journey, said to have been intoxicated, allowed ice to form in the cans and many perished by the time they arrived at the hatchery in Newcomb. William held the Caledonia supplier blameless and said he hoped to get some landlocked salmon at another time.

Archer Huntington occupied the Arbutus camp with his first wife, Helen Gates Huntington. In 1923 he married Anna Vaughn Hyett (1876–1973), a sculptor whose statues and smaller pieces were placed in public squares and in many museums and galleries in the U.S. One of the buildings at the camp was used by Mrs. Huntington as a studio. She modeled from deer kept on the property, and she and her husband, a poet and philanthropist, were said to have strong attachments to the natural environment. In 1932 they gave 13,000 acres of forest lands and lakes to the State University of New York. To this was added, in 1939, another 2,000 acres which included the Arbutus Lake Preserve and its camp. In 1951 they gave Camp Pine Knot to the State University of New York at Cortland.

Today the SUNY College of Environmental Science and Forestry conducts research on wildlife and forestry at what is variously known as the Adirondack Ecological Center and the Archer and Anna Huntington Wildlife Forest Station. Selective cutting of timber by the college provides income which supports the scientists and their projects at the research station. The camp buildings have been used for conferences and by visiting scientists and

138

students. William West Durant's plans for developing Newcomb into a second resort kingdom were obviously dashed by events that followed Collis P. Huntington's death in August, 1900. His lands on Rich Lake and on Goodenow Mountain were among those given by Mr. and Mrs. Archer Huntington to the State University of New York.

William's Fall   12

William West Durant's kingdom was nearly intact with the opening of the Raquette Lake Railroad in 1900. Collis P. Huntington had lent him money and muscle with which to deal with the other wealthy men who had invested in the region — J. Pierpont Morgan, Dr. William Seward Webb and William C. Whitney. The Eagle's Nest Country Club was open for members (Fig. 34), and the lands along and near Blue Mountain Lake had been divided into lots for sale to builders of summer cottages. But the tide was running against Durant, and he would soon be carried out to sea, like a mariner on a raft looking at the receding shore of a promised land.

The railroad, on which construction began in 1899, was more important to Durant than it was to the other men, who were as interested in having easier access to their camps as they were in making an investment. Huntington referred to the 18-mile Raquette Lake Railroad as "this little road," which it was when compared with the railroads that he, Morgan and Webb controlled. Durant may have proposed the railroad to Huntington, who objected to continuing the journey to camp from the Clearwater Station over a bumpy road.

The chief investors in the Raquette Lake Railroad were Huntington, who was president and paid $71,000; Morgan and William Seward Webb, at $70,000 apiece; William C. and H. C. Whitney, at $35,000; plus four other subscribers, including, possibly, Durant, at $1,000 each. Huntington was in charge. His brother-in-law, Isaac Edwin Gates, was appointed trustee for all the shares. The arrangement, according to Webb's manager in Herkimer, would "place all the stock in the hands of the persons desired by Mr. Huntington. . . ." For the first time since his father's death, William's role was more like that of a manager than an executive, no longer making decisions but waiting for them to be made by others.

Opponents of the railroad, some of whom owned camps near the proposed route, alleged that it would add to the fire hazard and was aimed at benefitting the logging interests. Senator Douglas, the owner of stumpage rights to nearby lands sold by Dr. Webb to the state, submitted enabling legislation in 1899, but it was not passed. Another effort was made on January 17, 1900, when Senator Raines introduced a bill waiving the statewide restriction against the operation of steam locomotion of street surface railroads, provided that oil was used to generate the steam. Durant lobbied in Albany for the act, but it was Lieutenant Governor Woodruff, a supporter of the idea since 1898, who won its passage. Durant telegraphed Huntington on April 5, "Bill passed Senate and Assembly just as you desired, owing at last moment to untiring efforts of Woodruff."

The confidence of the railroad's backers in this outcome is shown by the fact that the track was being laid the previous summer. By early August, 1899 Edward M. Burns was driving the crew at a furious pace, attempting to find 200 to 300 more men, to work at night, if necessary, so the railroad would be finished in time for Huntington's and Morgan's visits to their camps later that month.

Huntington and his partners were inclined to view the railroad's critics as the "sentimental opposition." Railroading meant progress, and they were convinced that the public eventually would allow barriers to development in the Adirondacks to be dropped. Huntington's attorney in Herkimer, Mr. C. E. Snyder (Fig. 33), told Durant that the state's amended Constitution of 1894 limited the old freedom with which trespasses on state land had been ignored or winked at. That is why, he said, the route preferred by William, to Raquette Lake at Sucker Brook Bay, was inadvisable, since it crossed state land in a corner of Township 41 [End Papers]. To stress this, he quoted Article 14 (the Forever Wild provision) of the Constitution and underlined the phrase, ". . . nor shall the timber thereon be sold, removed or destroyed."

If Durant, Huntington and the others could not readily accept the ban on removal of a few trees, it was because they foresaw a time when the timber-rich lands throughout the Raquette Lake region, estimated by Burns to hold 700,000,000 feet of spruce, would be opened for harvesting. In anticipation of this, their layout for the railroad terminal on Raquette Lake included, alongside a spur, a "ditch for floating logs." Proposals for cutting timber on some of the state's lands were being considered at this time. In 1901, the U.S. Department of Agriculture issued working plans for cutting timber in Townships 5, 6, 40 and 41, notwithstanding New York's Constitution and its provision against any removal of timber from the Forest Preserve.

When Collis P. Huntington died at Camp Pine Knot on August 13, 1900, Durant's fate was sealed. As Harold K. Hochschild wrote, "The bells that tolled Huntington's death sounded the knell of what was left of Durant's Adirondack empire." Huntington had agreed to an extension of time on a loan to Durant, but William, reminding Brother Gates of this shortly after Huntington's death, learned that Gates would not deal with him. Dr. Webb and William C. Whitney also refused to assist Durant. Soon the Huntington estate would call in the mortgages it held against the Forest Park and Land Company's properties.

In December, 1900 Durant went to Morgan for help. He offered to sell 3,000 shares or 60 percent of the capital stock of the FP&LC for $400,000, of which $360,000 would be used to pay off the company's indebtedness; the balance was for completing Durant's steamboat line, the golf course, a cottage, and to provide operating expenses until earnings from land sales and services started coming in the next summer. He told Morgan that he needed $60,000 immediately, another $50,000 in January and $50,000 in February. He asked Morgan to speak in his behalf, without delay, to the executor of the Huntington estate, Charles H. Tweed. On February 19, 1901, William wrote Tweed, "We can do nothing," meaning that money was needed to prepare for the next tourist season, at which Tweed dropped Morgan a note saying that Durant would submit to any course Morgan chose. Durant was trapped between Morgan and Tweed.

On March 16, Morgan offered to lend up to $350,000 to the FP&LC provided that he receive sixty percent of the capital shares in the company and the right to select the executive officers and board of directors. Durant replied that this was tantamount to giving Morgan sixty percent of the stock for nothing and an advantageous loan besides. It was, he said characteristically, like being "asked to shut my eyes and open my mouth without knowing what will be thrown into it." Tweed, negotiating for the Huntington estate, said that the management of the company would not be in Durant's hands and that no assurances could be given him as to his position or salary.

Durant's state of mind can be imagined from his letter to Morgan, dated March 18:

For twenty years I have worked hard and planned and succeeded in developing this property and region, and my interest in it is all that I now have. Mr. Tweed remarked to me Saturday that my 'good taste' in building would be recognized by the administration under new control.

Surely, Mr. Morgan, it required something more than 'good taste' to bring about, as I did, the building of the Raquette Lake Railway and the opening of this wilderness by steamboats, coach, the building of hotels, churches and roads, and the construction of the three best known and finest camps in the Adirondacks — Uncas, Sagamore and Pine Knot.

In July, 1901, Durant sold 34,135 acres of timber lands to the Raquette Falls Land Company for $150,000. The Sagamore Preserve, its buildings and contents were sold to Alfred G. Vanderbilt for $162,500. About $200,000 of this, plus interest, was used to pay off the mortages held by the Huntington estate, which had filed an action against the FP&LC in June. Harold K. Hochschild could not find where the remaining $100,000 went, but the Price-Waterhouse accounting of the preceding December showed $418,722 owed by Durant, through the FP&LC, so the remainder quickly disappeared into the pockets of William's fifty or so employees, on unfinished projects at Eagle's Nest and elsewhere, to say nothing of the fees owed to his lawyers for their continuing services in his sister's suit against him.

Two days after the Huntington estate cancelled its lien, Durant was forced to mortgage the remaining assets of the FP&LC for $100,000 to a trustee representing other creditors of the company. A year and a half later, on February 2, 1903, this group foreclosed and was awarded a judgment of approximately $109,000 the following October. This foreclosure may have been spurred by the $756,000 judgment made by the referee in favor of William's sister earlier that year.

William was no longer president or director of the Forest Park and Land Company, having been disqualified as early as January 26, 1903. He was appointed general manager at a monthly salary of $100, but this was soon reduced to $50, until October 1, when the company held its last meeting. On April 4, 1904, the remaining assets of the FP&LC, mostly lands on and near the Eckford Chain of lakes, passed into the hands of the Blue Mountain Land Company, which immediately began to dispose of them. The group of buyers included the father of Harold K. Hochschild, author of *Township 34* and the person chiefly responsible for the founding of the Adirondack Museum.

William lost his transportation system, as well. In 1901, it consisted of six steamboats, a naphtha launch, two scows, a derrick, a dredge, two car floats, a number of docks, boat houses and other buildings, plus the Marion River Carry Railroad with its locomotive, now on display at the Adirondack Museum (Figs. 37-1,2,3), and passenger and baggage cars. The system had been taken over in the spring of 1902 and renamed the Raquette Lake Transportation Company by a group headed by Dr. William Seward Webb. Unable to raise the $60,000 needed to retain equity in it, William lost the line as well. On May 10, 1902, he wired a former employee to say that he would not have himself seen buying a ticket when he came up the next week, and, as he did not know whether Dr. Webb intended to give him the customary free pass dispensed to people of consequence, he would appreciate having the matter looked into and reported back to him.

It is difficult to explain the frantic pace with which William assumed new commitments before resolving the old ones during the last five years of the century. Among all his projects, the camps were the greatest drain on his resources, since each required large outlays of cash which could not be repaid until they were furnished and ready for occupancy, down to wood in the fireplaces. Years later, in an interview with Hochschild, he admitted that the camps, for which he had become famous, always cost more than they were sold for. His upbringing, he said, had not prepared him to be a practical businessman. Hochschild believes that Durant found his real talent in building these elaborate lodges in the forest, and that he enjoyed the excitement, challenge and recognition that each afforded.

Hindsight impels us to ask why William did not try to develop his property on Blue Mountain Lake sooner. Plans were drawn about 1899–1900 which indicate his intention to sell or lease small plots of land around the lake to people of modest means, a market which held reasonable hope of financial success. On September 18, 1900, he wrote his harried superintendent, J. George Thompson, to say that Mr. Trotter, a Philadelphian interested in two lots on Blue Mountain Lake, must build his camp inside of a year, since "our object in selling these lots is to promptly see a development of the property." The north shore of Rich Lake in Newcomb was similarly divided in anticipation of a development for summer camps, further evidence that William counted on these sales and the subsequent business they would generate, in the way of transportation, construction, materials and other services which he would provide, to retrieve his fortunes in the Adirondacks. On August 31 he wrote Brother Gates, "With the building up of camps around Blue Mountain Lake, which is almost certain to come, and the opening up of the Indian Lake, Newcomb and Long Lake territories, the [railroad] will have a business that one . . . would scarcely believe possible."

As seen, however, William had chosen instead to concentrate valuable time and money on building grand camps for the rich and powerful. Perhaps he felt that their patronage was essential in bringing the railroad to Raquette Lake, and that their presence in the region, at residences already favorably portrayed in periodicals, would inspire confidence among thousands of prospering middle class families to emulate the Huntingtons, Morgans and Woodruffs by investing in second homes of their own. Mary F. Henderson, the wife of a former U.S. Senator from Missouri and owner of a camp on Indian Point on Raquette Lake, wrote William on January 2, 1899 to decline his invitation to put money in the proposed Raquette Lake Railroad, but closed with the consoling thought, "You have succeeded admirably in getting desirable and rich people in the woods, and I look forward to new and splendid projects for the advancement of the Raquette." We might say that William made a simple error in business judgment. He should have undertaken his more popular schemes for land development before embarking on building his grand camps.

But the error was not a simple matter. William was a masterful manager and a tireless worker. He went into the woods to survey boundaries, supervised construction of roads and buildings, the laying out of a golf club and dredging of channels for steamboats, and even taught Mary Callahan some cooking tricks in the kitchen. While these are the marks of an eminently practical man, we need look no further than his yacht *Utowana* for evidence of a different sort. His preference for people of wealth and social standing, for clubs and luxurious residential hotels in the city, reflects a taste with which most of us can identify given William's background and the fortune that passed into his hands in 1889. But a yacht costing over $200,000 with its inordinately high continuing cost for crew, operation and maintenance, can only be described as a measure of William's soaring ambition, not necessarily the source of his downfall, but symptomatic of the flaw of character that could have led him to embark on the construction of woodland palaces for the few rather than lakefront cottages for the many. By 1900 William was attempting to remedy that neglect, but events overtook him when Collis P. Huntington died at Camp Pine Knot on August 13, and the pieces of his elaborate Adirondack kingdom that he and his father had laboriously started to assemble more than twenty-five years earlier slipped inexorably from his control, one by one, into the hands of his creditors. By 1904 he had moved out of the Adirondacks and would henceforth be merely a visitor to the region, no longer a force in shaping its destiny.

The Later Years   13

The first six years after his departure from the Adirondacks were probably the worst of William's life. Then in his fifties, he was, in the words of Maurice Callahan, "tied to the chariot of his conquerors," an apt allusion to the humiliation of Hektor in the ancient Greek epic of honor, passion and war, "The Iliad." In 1904–1905 he was living in Utica. A year or two later he married Annie Cotton, a Canadian and his junior by twenty-three years, and they moved to Washington, D.C. where he attempted, unsuccessfully, to work in the optical business. He returned to the Adirondacks where he managed the Long View House in Long Lake in 1907 and the Lake Harris House in Newcomb in 1908. He was hired by a former employee, and Callahan remarked that some of the people who had worked for him went out of their way to see him and thereby assuage old grudges at his expense. He attempted to raise mushrooms in Portland, Maine in 1909–1910, but this too was a failure.

His life improved somewhat in 1910 when he was appointed "policy manager" for a development on Long Island called Jamaica Estates. A promotional photograph, later illustrated in *Township 34*, shows Durant standing among a group of newspapermen. The only other conspicuous figure among the sixteen is that of Timothy L. Woodruff, the president of the development, who may have repaid any lingering obligation to William by hiring him at a time of need. William resigned in 1913 when a financial panic halted work on the project.

During the years of World War I, William undertook title searches of lands in the Adirondacks and collected affidavits and other evidence for the continuing lawsuit between the Ladew family and New York State over ownership of Osprey Island. He did this for Charles E. Snyder, the Herkimer attorney involved with the opening of the Raquette Lake Railroad in 1899. He carried out similar searches for George Ostrander, the Glens Falls lawyer who had acquired some of Durant's lands. These jobs offered only occasional income, but the Ladew case took William back to old haunts and acquaintances on Raquette Lake (**Fig. 24**), perhaps indicating that he at last had come to terms with the past.

His second marriage was a happy one, according to Harold K. Hochschild. Annie Durant owned and ran a boarding house in New York City. A story in *The New York Times* for March 17, 1926 reported that William was "now employed in the real estate brokerage business conducted by his wife." The couple were paid a visit by Harold and Walter Hochschild in 1928 and invited to stay at what had been William's country club and golf course on Eagle Lake. In October, 1931, the Durants were guests at Eagle Nest, during which they saw Camp Uncas (**Fig. 25**) and other of William's projects. The notes taken by Harold K. Hochschild during his conversations, together with photographs and other materials received later from members of the Durant family, were used in the writing of *Township 34*, a book published in 1952 and dedicated by Hochschild to William West Durant.

William died at Mount Sinai hospital on June 1, 1934 at the age of 83, following an operation. Two years later, on August 12, 1936, his widow unveiled a stone and bronze marker dedicated to him for "developing the Adirondacks and making known their beauty." The marker, installed by the New York State Department of Education, was opposite the lake formed by a Civilian Conservation Corps dam built two years earlier. The lake was christened Lake Durant, and it and the memorial may be seen today by travellers on the highway two miles east of the village of Blue Mountain Lake.

Before his death and even after it, people believed that William had retained rights to timber and water of certain properties in the Adirondacks. Ella, convinced this was so, renewed her lawsuit on March 17, 1926, asking for a total of $2,076,000 from her brother. William replied that he had no money and that he had been unable to enter into business because of her claims against him. The matter of Heloise Durant Rose versus William West Durant was officially laid to rest on June 13, 1927 when a deed was recorded in the Hamilton County clerk's office settling four-fifths of whatever rights William still held in the Adirondacks on his sister. Ella then wrote an official of the state, on stationery of the Dante Society of America, asking for assistance in determining the value of what she had acquired. The reply, if any, is not known, but Ella, who had been told by her father that she would have a cottage and a lake of her own in the Adirondacks some day, got nothing. William's second wife, who held the remaining one-fifth interest, believed that he had reserved the water rights in some early deeds. Writing Mr. Snyder on June 19, 1937, she hopefully recalled, "Mr. Durant often said the water at some future time for New York City would be brought from Raquette & other lakes — he always visioned things of that sort but was ahead of his time."

The other members of the Durant family, some of whom were participants in a drama in which they wanted no part, disappeared with little or no trace. Mrs. Thomas Clark Durant died in Utica in January, 1901, before she could witness the collapse of the family's fortunes and reputation. A story bearing a Utica dateline reported that her personal effects had been appraised at less than $2,000 and sold. Janet Stott Durant, William's first wife, lived in New York City following her divorce in 1898; she died in 1931 and was buried in Stockport, N.Y., near her childhood home. Of their three children, the second, Heloise or "Lella" Seeley (1887–1964), supplied much of the information about her family in the *Durant Genealogy* and gave many photographs and other memorabilia, besides those from Annie Durant, which were used in the preparation of this book. She was present at the dedication of the memorial to her father on Lake Durant in 1936.

Ella, William's sister, was described as an "author and dramatist" in a story in an 1899 issue of the *New York Daily Tribune* telling of her successful suit. A picture (Fig. 22) showed her with her three year old son, Timbrell Durant Rose (1896–1962). By the turn of the century she had published *Pine Needles or Sonnets and Songs* (1884), a book of lyric poems; *Dante, A Dramatic Poem* (eds. 1889, 1892, 1910), a play in verse (see Appendix A); and a novel of manners set in London, *A Ducal Skeleton* (1899). She contributed literary pieces and criticism to newspapers in New York City, and an announcement in one, on April 19, 1908, said that her play "Dante" would probably be staged in Venice and possibly in Paris. Other than this little is known of Ella's later life. In 1926 she was living in New City, Rockland County, though she wrote she could be reached in nearby New York City at the National Arts Club or through the Dante Society, of which she was vice president and secretary. She was alive on June 19, 1937, when Annie Durant wrote, ". . . I have NO wish to communicate in *any* way with Mrs. Rose, who was largely responsible for ruining Mr. Durant's business life & causing trouble to all her family." Ella got far less space in the *Durant Genealogy* than her son, a businessman, and she got none at all in the marble tomb built for the family in Green Wood Cemetery in 1871 (Fig. 26).

William's pride was a defect, but it also must have been his salvation after the crushing defeats he suffered at the hands of his creditors and sister. He never lost the dignity and reserve that quickly established his character to those who met him for the first time. Photographs in later life show him impeccably dressed in business suits and starched shirts, resolutely but not stiffly posed as if to invite the camera or viewer to find the slightest sign of weakness or regret. He was a man who, after all, had entertained the future King of England and other members of European royalty on his own yacht. Most of the people who worked for William admired and respected him. Maurice Callahan, looking back more than fifty years to the time when he was an employee at Pine Knot, admitted that Durant was hard to get along with, particularly during the difficult period at the end of the century, but "I always regarded [him] as a wonderful man . . . a great man to teach a person; I learned more from this man than any man living. He was a driver, but he had a great heart."

William was stung by his sister's imputations on his character, and he was so strong in his denial of them that one believes he must have thought himself largely innocent of her charges. He was the end product of a free-wheeling, materialistic age that professed adherence to discarded values. He had followed his father's example of consolidating the estate within the family and its loyal associates. Ella inspired little confidence that she could be enlisted in the task of concentrating resources and selling to advantage, so that each transaction would add to what had gone before, like the pieces of a jigsaw puzzle falling into place to form an emerging picture. Still, his failure to treat his sister fairly or seriously was a profound mistake.

Durant's breadth of view, encompassing a territory the size of a small state, was not to be duplicated until the arrival of scientific planners to the region in the 1960's. He knew the lay of the land, its forest cover and how its waters ran. He permitted logging, but he was aware that this took management and care. He helped to build a transportation system which made getting to the Adirondacks by public transit easier in 1900 than it is today. The environmental ethic holds sway over much of the region, assuring protection of the natural beauty of the Adirondacks for many years to come. But it is arguable whether the emphasis on the environment has not been accompanied by a contraction in those services and features which made the Adirondack experience a richly social and personal event for thousands of people at the turn of the century. The experiences of today's visitors may be said to be different, but they cannot be said to be more varied or civilizing than they were when the guiding hand and intelligence of William West Durant were at work in the last quarter of the nineteenth century.

Sources

The best history of the central Adirondacks and the Durants is (1) Harold K. Hochschild, *Township 34*, N.Y.: Privately printed, 1952. My treatment supplements Hochschild's book, it does not supplant it. The research notes for *Township 34*, large parts of which were reissued as booklets by the Adirondack Museum, were also consulted. They are in the Museum's library together with most of the other sources cited below.

The transcripts of testimony and legal briefs produced from the suit brought by Heloise against her brother are the most important:

(2) Supreme Court, Appellate Division, First Department, *Heloise D. Rose against William W. Durant, Papers on Appeal from Order Adjudging Defendant in Contempt*, N.Y., 1901, 60 pp.

(3) _____ , *Brief for Defendant and Appellant on Appeal from Order Adjudging Him in Contempt of Court*, N.Y., n.d., 32 pp.

(4) _____ , *Brief for Appellant*, N.Y., n.d., 72 pp.

(5) _____ , *Case on Appeal, Vol. I, Record of Trial at Special Term*, N.Y., 1903, 572 pp.

Item (5) is by far the most informative, consisting largely of testimony recorded during the trial in January, 1899.

Further information about the Durant family was gleaned from a variety of sources:

(6) *The Durant Genealogy:* Vol. I, Compiled to 1890 by the Rev. William Durant and Continued in Part by His Great Nephew, Alexander G. Rose, III. Baltimore, Md., Privately printed, 1966.

Vol. II, *Ibid.*, 1968.

A sympathetic biographical sketch of Dr. Durant, by General Silas Seymour, a consulting engineer for the Union Pacific and an associate of the doctor's, is an item of interest in Volume I.

(7) Letter books, personal correspondence, maps, other materials relating to William West Durant and the Durant family, in the archives of the library at the Adirondack Museum.

(8) Correspondence relating to William West Durant among the Collis P. Huntington collection, George Arents Research Library for Special Collections, Syracuse University.

(9) Articles in newspapers in New York City and Brooklyn, N.Y., particularly *The New York Times*.

The Adirondack Museum owns numerous photographs depicting the Durants, their camps, the North Creek home of Dr. Durant and William's yacht *Utowana*. These were given to the museum, with other memorabilia, by several members of the Durant family. An impression of Dr. Durant's achievement in building the Union Pacific Railroad may be gained by examining the illustrated book by Barry B. Combs, *Westward to Promontory*, N.Y., Garland, 1969.

Anyone studying the uses and abuses of land transactions in the Adirondacks should begin with the reports issued by various commissions of New York State. For the period covered in *Durant*, see (10) Verplanck Colvin, *First Annual Report of the Commissioners of State Parks*, Albany, Weed, Parsons, 1874. Also: (11) *First Annual Report of the Forest Commission of the State of New York . . . 1885*, Albany, Argus, 1886, and reports for subsequent years. The names of the commissions changed: e.g., the reports between 1895 and 1899 were issued by the Fisheries, Game and Forest Commission, between 1900 and 1910 by the Forest, Fish and Game Commission, etc.

Testimony relating to land in Raquette Lake, in the form of published transcripts and unpublished affidavits, constitute an immensely valuable and entertaining source of historical information:

> (12) Supreme Court, Appellate Division, Third Division *The People of the State of New York Against Jennie H. Ladew and Joseph H. Ladew, Case on Appeal*, Walton, N.Y., 1920.
>
> (13) _____ , *People of the State of New York Against George H. Carlin, Cooperstown, N.Y.* [c. 1919].
>
> (14) _____ , *People of the State of New York vs. Earl J. Blanchard* [and others]. *Appellant's Brief and Respondent's Brief*, Batavia, N.Y. [1952].

The Ladew action (12) dated from September 1, 1897, when the state issued a warning of trespass. The Carlin suit, involving Hunter's Rest Camp on Constable Point, seems to date from 1904, though (13) dates from the time of the defendant's appeal, August 21, 1919. These and other suits brought by the state were eventually won by the occupants of lands claimed by the state. Many of the papers of Charles E. Snyder, who was Ladew's lawyer, are in the library at the Adirondack Museum.

(15) Attempts to gain the assistance of New York State in building a railroad through the Adirondacks are clearly outlined in a succession of nine descriptive pamphlets issued between 1864 and 1883 by the Adirondack Company. One, for example, is titled, "An Argument Showing Why the State Should Aid in the Construction of a Railroad Through the Wilderness of Northern New York," Albany, 1870. These and other documents on railroading, some of which belonged to the Durant family, are in the vertical file at the Adirondack Museum library under "Railroads."

Two recent books of value are (16) Roger C. Thompson, *The Doctrine of Wilderness: A Study of the Policy and Politics of the Adirondack Preserve-Park*, 2 vols., Syracuse State University College of Forestry at Syracuse University, 1962, and (17) Norman J. VanValkenburgh, *The Adirondack Forest Preserve*, The Adirondack Museum, 1979. The first is a doctoral thesis, the second a narrative of the evolution in the Forest Preserve, originally issued in multilithed form in 1968.

Appendices

APPENDIX A

In 1881 Ella went to Cambridge, Massachusetts, where she showed her "dramatic poem" about Dante, in manuscript, to Henry Wadsworth Longfellow. She may have been a member of the group that formed the Dante Society, which still exists, in Cambridge that year. Her work, a play in verse, was published with the title *Dante, A Dramatic Poem* in London in 1889 and again in 1892 and 1910, when it was being considered for production in Europe. The "Proem" below is her dedication to the 14th century Italian poet in the book.

To Dante

Thou mighty poet-king, with brows thrice crowned
By genius, sorrow, love, who darest express
Thy scathing thoughts aloud when bitterness
Possessed thy soul; whom Florence once disowned,
Denied to sing or live; who now sits throned
In every heart through Italy, no less
Revered than loved; who spiest each dark recess
And uncouth horror of the abyss profound,
O look not thou reprovingly on me
For stretching feeble wings towards eagle height,
Wresting thy utterance, depicting thee
With my poor pencil. Infants turn to light;
And so my weakness seeks thy strength to touch.
Dante! though frail my art, my love is much.

[Heloise Durant]

APPENDIX B

Excerpts in various hands from the Diary kept at Camp Stott, Raquette Lake, N.Y., August 18, 1876–September 19, 1900. Adirondack Museum Library, Gift of Mrs. Bromley Seeley.

[1878] Rev. Mr. Noble held first service on the Lake in our camp. Aug. 11th, 1878.

[1880] W. W. Durant. My first call!!!
First service held in Church, Aug. 29th. Consecration by Bishop Doane, Sept. 12th.

[1881] Spinsterage first occupied this summer.

[1882] Annex to Spinsterage built this year.

[1884] July 16th. Mrs. F. H. Stott, Miss Janet Stott and Wm. W. Durant. Remained only a few hours. Returned to B. M. [Blue Mountain Lake] the same afternoon.

Boat House was built this year.

[1885] New house built by [Nelson] Morehouse, occupied by gentlemen. Bath house and laundry were built and occupied this summer.

[1886] July 31st. F. H. Stott visited Camp with Mr. Thomas Wallace, Builder, and then and there decided to remove the old building and put up on same ground a rustic log house. The Spinsterage which was built and occupied in 1882 will also be removed.

Aug. 21st. The old house was down, and foundation for new one nearly laid. Mr. Wallace and family were occupying the Spinsterage.

Sept. 4. All went over to Camp Stott [the family stayed at Pine Knot during construction at Bluff Point] and inspected buildings. Foundations were ready and floor timbres of main house being laid.

[1887] May 10th. Arrived at Camp Stott about six p.m., taking possession of the new house and eating supper there.

May 17th. Tuesday. Party all left camp, leaving the two gentlemen at Pine Knot. The weather during this visit was very warm and dry. No rain falling; large fires in the woods making the atmosphere misty and smokey.

Guides for 1887. Joe O. A. Bryere, Willard Locke, Frank Emerson, Dennis Mahan from Troy. Aug. 30th, Sid Porter for Brown's Tract Camp. Sept. 20th, Jerome Wood for the hunt, John Ballard for the hunt, Ike Kenwell started dogs.

Sept. 11th "The last night in Camp
How dreadful the sound,
But one thing consoles us,
Next year's coming 'round."

[1889] The annual Entertainment for the "Church of the Good Shephard" was held at Camp Stott on the afternoon of August 22nd. About one hundred people came. Miss Oakley had charge of the Fancy Table in the main house, Miss Clara the Dining Fly [i.e., tent] with refreshments, Miss Louise & Mr. Berlin in the Gypsy House where Miss Stott told fortunes. Mr. Williams, Mr. Louie Stott were on the Reception Committee. The amount realized clear of expenses was $300.00. The Song of the Open Camp . . . was sung by some of the young people. It was written

150

out on a large sheet of birch bark, [which] was afterwards sold at auction and bought by Col. Shepard of New York for $30.00.

[1890] Sunday, May 14th. Warm and pleasant. Mr. W. W. Durant dined at camp. Then Mrs. Stott went with him and inspected Church and new additions to the Rectory. Took supper at Pine Knot.

July 5th. J. O. A. Bryere & family left camp and Mr. Henry Brown of Indian Lake arrived to take charge.

Hisaya Iwasaki, Japan. [Signature.]

[1891] May 15th. R. C. Church dedicated. [St. Williams Roman Catholic Church] Guides all went. Pleasant day. More fishing.

Sep. 2nd. Telegram received that the Yacht "Utowana" sailed from Boston today direct for the Azores.

Sep. 7th. Spent morning in packing trunks. Rev. Mr. Mulford came on steamer for dinner. Afternoon the ladies walked on Brandreth Carry and fished for bass.

Sep. 8th. Last day at camp for this year. At ten o'clock a deer was seen swimming from Bluff Point across to Indian Point. Willard & Mr. Louis went out in a boat and shot it. Great excitement in the camp about it.

[1892] After tea all went out in the barge, sailing around, singing and enjoying the bright moonlight. Gave the Rectory people a seranade, to which they responded with great enthusiasm.

Dec. 20. Arrived at Camp Pine Knot, having driven from Roblee's at North River in a sleigh that day.

Sunday, Dec. 25. Christmas day. Snowy and cold. Mercury fell to 15 below zero at night.

Dec. 27. The supper for guides, residents and their families was held in John McLoughlin's house. Then all went to the work shop for the tea and dance afterwards. About sixty persons were present. It was a splendid clear cold moonlight night and every one enjoyed the festivities. [A band from Lake George furnished the music.]

Jan. 3, 1893. Party all down in sleighs to Lake Shedd [Sagamore] and Lake Mohegan, only the second time the horses had crossed the carry to the last place. A picnic in the snowy forest. A snow shoe walk on the lake and a decision for a camp site [for Camp Uncas].

[1894] Aug. 9. Went to camp on Sumner [Kora] with two guides, Cornell and John Gerald. Remained that night. On Friday went to Sumner outlet, a two mile tramp, fished for brook trout and in 4½ hours caught *ninety-five.*

Aug. 11, Saturday. Walked to Mohegan for dinner. Then all this camp party returned home. Mr. & Mrs. Durant and Dr. Pratt walking with them to Shedd [Sagamore] camp. Had tea.

Aug. 29. In afternoon every one in camp but Mrs. S., Mr. Louis, the cow and the cat went to the R. C. Fair held at Hemlocks [hotel] to witness the boat and log races. The young men took the Barge out for the first time this season.

Oct. 2nd. Our tomato vines still untouched [by frost]. This is the first season we have gathered from them sufficient for our table salads. Party all took dinner at Pine Knot, a farewell feast. Dr. Pratt there also. W. W. D. has been in N.Y. for past three weeks.

[1895] Sept. 1st. All felt as lazy as possible, realizing it was one last Sunday in camp. The moonlight and open camp were more than enjoyed in the evening. Then the maidens gathered around the fire side and talked until after midnight, ensconsed in easy chairs and loose flowing garments.

[1896] Oct. 3. Henry Brown [caretaker at camp through Oct. 3] came at nine and was finished at camp by four. Every closet has been cleared out, old things discarded, inventory taken, blankets and rugs put away, storm shutters placed on windows of main house. As the place will be left unoccupied this winter, Charles Pashley [?] of Deerhurst was engaged to overlook it occasionally and fill the ice house.

[In 1896 the family returns to Stottville by way of the Fulton Chain and Utica rather than North Creek and Saratoga as they had done in previous years.]

[1898] The camp was occupied this summer by Mrs. Lucy Carnegie and family from Fernandina, Fla. They remained until October. George Jenkins remained until Jan. 10th, 1899 and with his brother cut 75 cords of wood for next season. Also built new out buildings, altered the cooler in the ice house.

[1899] May 23. Flower beds were prepared for seeds, linen closet put in order, blankets and pillows aired. P. M. the ladies went fishing. Mrs. S. caught five Lakers by trolling and Miss M. five brook trout in Stillman Bay. A beautiful calm day, lake so quiet and coloring of hills & mountains grand.

June 2nd. Mrs. S., Miss M. and I went to Church Island. Pipes were connected, house [the rectory] was opened, flower seeds planted. Then to P.O. for mail. After tea, ladies went fishing.

June 3rd. Work on drain progressing. George burning up refuse piles.

June 7. Ladies packed, spent most of the day indoors on account of black flies & mosquitos.

August 24. George Jenkins came from B.M. [Blue Mountain Lake] and moved his family away.

August 25. I put away Blankets and prepared for winter. Had the old outhouse burned. The whole camp has a most neglected and uncared for look. G. J. [George Jenkins] not having attended to it as he was engaged to do.

Sunday, Aug. 29th. A still quiet day. All went to the 10 o'clock services. Bishop Satterlee of Washington administered communion there at 11. Mrs. Bonchee was the only person I knew. Old times came crowding back in my thoughts. It was almost too sad. We dined at the "Antlers" [hotel] and then called on Mrs. Worthington. Home by 6 p.m.

August 30. Packed and put away everything. Shutters on windows, took up pipes. Left on line boat at 1:30. W. R. Bates is engaged for a year to take care of camp.

[1900] May 29. Left Stockport at 8 a.m., took Empire State at 11. Changed at Utica and again at Clear Water. There took the new railroad and arrived at Raquette Lake at 5 p.m.

152

August 14. We heard of death of C. P. Huntington at Pine Knot last evening.

August 16. Mr. Collier finished tuning piano. Games in house in evening.

September 19. All left for home. . . . Party separated at Albany. A glorious [day?] which ends this book.

Editor's Note: Except for humorous and sentimental verses by family and guests in the back pages, the entry above concluded the 24-year chronicle of Camp Stott. In 1910 the camp was sold to the magazine publisher, Robert Collier.

APPENDIX C

In this letter, Collis P. Huntington, the president and chief stockholder of the Raquette Lake Railway Company, expresses views about the future prospects for the central Adirondack region that were influenced by William West Durant. Burns was the general manager for the railroad.

23 Broad Street
New York, November 20/99

Mr. E. M. Burns,
    Herkimer, N.Y.

My dear Sir: —

I have your letter of the 10th, with newspaper clippings enclosed and note contents of all. One of the clippings shows a little animus against the Raquette Lake Railway Co., but I think such articles will not do any harm; in fact, I think they will do good, as they will put people on inquiry, and in that way they will find out about this little [rail]road and whether it will be likely to harm or help the public. In my opinion, it will help one hundred for every one it will discommode. In fact, I do not believe it will harm anyone unless it may possibly be the owners of the little steamers which ply on the Fulton Chain of Lakes, from whom I see you think the opposition comes. No doubt those boats will lose some of their through business, for people who want to visit the beautiful country lying to the eastward of those lakes will hardly care to take the old inconvenient and uncomfortable route, when an infinitely better way is available. Under the old arrangement, the traveler had to leave the great Central Road at Fulton Chain Station, take a little two-mile railroad up to Old Forge; there change to one of the little lake boats, transferring baggage and summer supplies as well; steam for an hour through the Chain until the east end of 4th Lake was reached; there the passenger and his baggage and stores were deposited on the wharf, transferred to wagons and pulled across a "Carry" to 5th Lake. There another little steamer was taken and baggage and supplies were put on board, and another hour was spent in steaming through 5th, 6th and 7th Lakes; again came a transfer of the passenger and his bag and baggage to wagons, and another ride to 8th Lake; here there was still another transfer to a third steamer, with baggage and stores, and when 8th Lake had been traversed again the passenger alighted with his baggage and was transported across another carry to Brown's Tract Inlet, where still another steamer awaited him; and after the seventh transfer of parcels and baggage had been made the traveler began a long, slow and tiresome trip through that narrow, shallow and tortuous little stream, the steamer often striking the bottom and running into the bank, long poles being used to push her off. At last the beautiful Raquette Lake was reached, after five hours or more of a journey which had for its only recommendation some charming scenery more than counter-balanced, after the novelty had worn off, by the discomfort and inconvenience attending antiquated and out-of-date methods.

It is hardly conceivable, of course, that anybody would voluntarily subject himself to such a trial when, by taking the Raquette Lake Railway route, he could remain comfortable in his seat in the railway coach and in one hour from the time he left Clearwater Station, on the main line, be at Raquette Lake itself. When the facilities to the eastward of Raquette Lake are improved, as they will be, then people who wish to spend a few days or a few weeks at any of the attractive Lakes of that region — such as Blue Mountain, Eagle, Utowana, Sagamore, Killkare, Mohican, Forked, Long and many others — can leave New York City in the morning of any long day in summer and before sundown can be at their destination.

You seem to think that, unless the Raquette Lake Railway Company will consent to buy these little steamers on the Fulton Chain of Lakes, the owners of them will strongly oppose the use by the Railway Company of the power that it should have the right to use — viz., steam. I cannot believe that there will be any such opposition, or, if there is, that the people will be influenced by it or patient under it. It is certain that the public will want the best and most economical power, for it is the public which will have to pay for it in the end. What the public demands is that the power that is used shall not be such as will harm their great park by setting fire to the woods, and no one would deprecate more than the writer of this the use of any power that would injure these beautiful forests which the Raquette Lake Railway will traverse. I think the great State of New York never enacted a wiser law than it did when it passed the act making the State a protector of this great preserve in which are located the sources of so many of our rivers and which will, by reason of the preservation of the forest, continue to feed our important streams in the future. It is a health resort for the rich and poor, for in these forests may be found the castle, the cabin and the tent, and the inmates of these share alike in the life-giving air of the woods. As I have said, the people themselves want the best facilities in the Adirondacks that they can possibly get, consistent with security to the forest itself, and I think there will be no other improvement in this grand lake country, in the way of transportation for persons and property, of the same length and cost as this little Raquette Lake railroad. It is now completed, and the question is: What should be the power to operate it? It is so short that the use of compressed air or electricity, which requires an expensive plant to compress the one or gather the other would be too costly, and, as I have before mentioned, this cost would necessarily react upon the patrons of the road, who are the real beneficiaries. Then again, if a different kind of power is employed from that used by the New York Central, passengers, instead of going straight from their homes to Raquette Lake without change, will be compelled to transfer or change cars at Clearwater Station, which is a thing they should not be required to do. In the dry lands west of the Rocky Mountains a light bituminous coal was used for perfect safety through the simple device of putting a wire screen of fine mesh over the smoke-stack of the locomotive. If the Raquette Lake Railway should be allowed to use anthracite, coke or oil, all possible danger would be obviated. The road runs for nearly its whole distance along a wagon road, and I am satisfied that the danger of fires from the carelessness of sportsmen, travelers and tramps, in building camp fires and throwing burning matches and lighted cigar stumps among the dried leaves is a hundred times greater than any danger to be apprehended from the fuel of a locomotive. Then, again, with a fire once started in these woods it is almost impossible to fight it successfully unless there is a railroad to take men to it. I have been told — no doubt truly — that several fires were started last summer along this line of road by others than the railroad people or their locomotives, and that it would have been practically impossible to extinguish them had it not been for the facility with which men were taken to the scene because of the existence of this railroad.

On the whole, therefore, I believe your apprehensions are not well founded, and that you will find among the people of the State more intelligence than you credit them with, when this question of the proper power employed under the simple precautions I have mentioned is the best for the people, and I have faith to believe that the people will so understand it.

I am,

Yours very truly

[Collis P. Huntington]

APPENDIX D

Inventory, Pine Knot
1895

SWISS COTTAGE

SITTING ROOM

1 Brown carpet
1 Large rug
1 Small rug
1 Piano
1 Sofa   5 Sofa pillows
1 Large arm chair
1 Rustic gun rack
1 Rustic standing lamp
2 Rustic tables
1 Rustic book case
2 Rocking chairs
1 Rustic armchair
2 Chairs
  Electric bell

1 Japanese Screen
1 Wire fire screen
2 Students lamps
1 Wood box (rustic)
1 Pair andirons
1 Iron fire fender
1 Set fire irons
1 Bellows
1 Portiere
4 Red curtains
4 Deer heads
1 Writing pad
1 Wooden letter paper rack
3 Stuffed birds   1 Rustic piano stool

RIGHT-HAND FRONT ROOM

1 Red carpet
1 Double rustic bed, with springs,
   hair mattress, and two pillows
2 Tables
1 Dressing stand
1 Toilet set
1 Foot tub
1 Tray with ice water pitcher
 and one glass

2 Chairs
1 Stove
1 Wood box
1 Mirror
2 Curtains (red)
2 Candle brackets
1 Lamp
1 Wicker clothes hamper

LEFT-HAND FRONT ROOM

1 Brown carpet
1 Double bed with springs, hair
   mattress and two pillows
1 Toilet set
1 Dressing stand
1 Table
2 Chairs
1 Washstand

1 Stove
1 Wood Box
1 Mirror
2 Candle brackets
2 Red Curtains
1 Lamp
1 Comode
1 Tray, with ice water pitcher and glass

BACK ROOM (Left-hand)

1 Red carpet
1 Single bed, with springs, hair
  mattress and pillow
2 Chairs
1 Bureau
1 Washstand

1 Toilet set
1 Mirror
2 Candle brackets
1 Lamp
2 Curtains
1 Water pitcher and glass on tray

BACK ROOM (Right-hand)

1 Carpet
1 Single bed, springs, hair mattress,
  cotton mattress and pillow
1 Chair
2 Curtains

1 Stove
1 Wood Box
1 Toilet set
1 Mirror
1 Lamp

HALL

1 Cocoa matting
2 Bracket lamps
1 Fire pail

UPPER WOOD SHED

1 Saw horse
1 Saw
1 Scuttle
1 Ash shovel
1 Broom

STORE ROOM

1 Coal stove
2 Fire pails
1 Chair
1 Clothes hamper

1 Piazza wicker sofa
1 Piazza rocking chair
1 Piazza arm chair

DINING ROOM

1 Rug
1 Extension table (10 leaves)
1 Stove
1 Wood Box
3 Lamps
1 Wicker screen

5 Pairs of Turkey-red curtains
18 Chairs
1 Towel rack
1 Clothes hamper
1 Japanese Screen
1 Butler's tray and stand

DINING ROOM PANTRY

18 Soup plates
24 Dinner plates
24 Breakfast plates
24 Desert plates
18 Fish plates
18 Salad plates
18 Preserve saucers
24 Coffee cups
24 Coffee saucers
24 Tea saucers
 6 Meat platters

24 After-dinner coffee cups (Dresden)
24 After-dinner saucers (Dresden)
18 Butter plates
8 Yellow bowls
3 Fancy china bowls
2 Fancy china tea pots
1 Fruit dish
2 Butter dishes
1 Egg stand (Dresden)
1 Mustard pot
2 Tile stands

1 Soup tureen
3 Salt cellars
1 Coffee pot
1 Small flat dish
6 Vegetable dishes

6 Pitchers
1 Glass lemon squeezer
4 Coffee filters
2 China soup ladles

GLASS

24 Water glasses
24 Champagne glasses
24 Sherry glasses
24 Claret glasses
24 Whiskey glasses
24 Liquor glasses
12 Vichey glasses
6 Salt shakers
12 Salt cups
8 Glass dishes
1 Champagne cutter

7 Glass pitchers
1 Glass Sugar bowl
8 Claret Decanters
5 Sherry Decanters
1 Vinegar cruet
1 Oil cruet
3 Sherry decanters
12 Egg glasses
1 Wooden bread board
1 Cork screw

SILVER

1 Wicker Silver basket containing

4 Doz. forks	4 Doz. knives	2 Butter knives
2 Doz. desert spoons	1 Soup ladle	3 Sets carvers
6 Doz. teaspoons	1 Gravy ladle	2 Steels
3 Doz. Table spoons	1 Fish set	1 Cocktail strainer
1 Wooden salad set	1 Mustard spoon	5 Trays 11 Glass cloths

LIST OF ARTICLES
OVER AND ABOVE THOSE CALLED FOR ON THE
PINE KNOT INVENTORY
LEFT FOR
MR. C. P. HUNTINGTON at PINE KNOT

SWISS COTTAGE
———

SITTING ROOM

| 2 Wrought iron lanterns | 1 Round Cushion | 1 Cushion filled with balsam |
| 1 Cuspidor | 1 Rustic Clock | 1 Piano Cover |

RIGHT-HAND FRONT ROOM

1 Sponge rack   1 Hot Water Can

LEFT-HAND FRONT ROOM

| 1 Hot water can | 3 Cans and Basket | 1 Pin Cushion |

BACK ROOM (Left hand)

2 Baskets   1 Pin Cushion   1 Hot Water Can

BACK ROOM (Right hand)   HALL

1 Hot Water Can

1 Red Curtain   1 Door Curtain

CLOSET

2 Tack Hammers
1 Carpet Sweeper
1 Carpet Stretcher
1 Pail
1 Slop Pail
4 Hot water Cans

STORE ROOM

12 Fans
20 Flower bulb glasses
2 Brass Candlesticks
8 Red Curtains
11 Dusting sheets
1 Comforter
1 Rubber Sheet
2 Dust Pans

STORE ROOM (Right hand)

10 Stone Jars with Covers
1 Small table
1 Step ladder
1 Twine Ball Case

BACHELORS' COTTAGE

2 Hot Water Cans
1 Rustic Clock

1 Cuspidor
1 Pin cushion

1 Wood Stove
3 Steel traps

MRS. W. W. DURANT'S HOUSE

SITTING ROOM

2 Chair-back Cushions
3 Pine Knot Mail-bags
2 Paper Baskets
1 Waste Paper Basket

1 Hanging Lamp
1 Large Blue Dish or Plate
1 Green plate
3 Cane Baskets

BED ROOM

2 Rustic Tables
1 Water Pitcher
2 Glasses and tray
2 Small cushions

1 Toasting Fork
2 Pillows
2 Stools

MRS. T. C. DURANT'S HOUSE

STOVE ROOM

1 Thermometer

1 Wood Stove
2 Sponge Baskets

BIG NURSERY

1 Copper Boiler
1 Window Sash Cushion
1 Sponge Rack
1 Hot Water Can
1 Small Clock

LONG NURSERY HALL

2 Red Curtains

SMALL NURSERY

1 Table Cover
1 Wood Stove
2 Green Window Cushions

160

GOVERNESS'S ROOM
3 Red Curtains

DINING ROOM

1 Crumb brush and tray
1 Hanging Lamp

3 Small tables
3 Wooden flower boxes

DINING ROOM PANTRY

12 Square fruit plates
10 Soup plates
1 Fruit Dish
3 Tea Pots
2 Butter chips (china)
8 Butter chips (glass)
3 Whisky glasses
18 Sherry glasses
37 Three-fourth Tumblers
2 Small vases
1 Tea cup & saucer
1 Vegetable dish covers
1 Rustic bottle

1 W Dinner Plate
3 Small pitchers
1 China Stand
1 Match Holder
1 Glass bowl
1 plated bell
1 Wire strainer
1 Cocktail shaker
2 Salt spoons
1 Wire strainer
2 Tea canisters
1 Sugar sifter

GLASS
Besides the glass inventoried, the following list of articles was purchased from Lewis & Conger, by W. W. Durant, for Pine Knot, July 5th, 1895.

2 Dozen Goblets
2 Dozen Champagne Tumblers
2 Dozen Tumblers
2 Dozen Clarets
2 Dozen Wines
1 Dozen Liquors
3 Glass Berry Bowls
1 Dozen Individual Salts
3 W. G. Slop Jars
1 Dec. Toilet Set
1 Glass Lemon Squeezer
6 Wood Spoons
2 Chop Trays
1 Jelly Bag
1 Pudding Mould
1 Set Skewers
1 Set larding needles

2 Ice picks
1 Atwater Ice cream freezer
4 P.M. Trays
2 Brown Coffee Biggins
3 Yellow Bowls
1 Soup Sieve
1 Tea Strainer
1 Agate Tea Pot
1 Agate Tea Kettle
1 Egg Whip
1 Egg Beater
6 Tin pies
8 Milk Pans
1 Cake Turner
1 Stove Brush
1 Black Lead Brush
2 Wire Brush Trays
2 Brooms

KITCHEN

1 Flour Scoop
9 Sauce pan covers
2 Baking tins

2 Copper Sauce pans
1 Copper stock pot
1 Copper braising pan

KITCHEN (Continued)

2 Agate spoons
1 Flour dredger
1 Iron Pot stand
1 Knife Box
1 Table spoon
9 Cake forms
1 Glass sugar bowl
2 Round agate pans
1 Garbage can
1 Steamer and pot (new)

1 Farina Kettle
1 Sauce pan
1 Broiling machine
7 Stone jars with covers
1 Potato scoop
6 Water tumblers
1 Brown jug
10 Roller towels
1 Clothes boiler (new)

MAIDS COTTAGE
———

WAITRESSES' ROOM

1 Single bed and springs and mattresses (2 pillows are in extras)

ICE HOUSE

1 Meat Block
1 Cleaver
2 Axes
1 Pair ice tongs
1 Scoop shovel

1 Candlestick
1 Meat saw
1 Steelyards
1 Thermometer
1 Pike pole

GUIDES' HOUSE: KITCHEN BUILDING
———

FRONT BED-ROOM

1 Pair red curtains

1 Bureau

BACK BED-ROOM

1 Chair

DINING ROOM

1 Wood box

1 Sideboard

KITCHEN

8 Kitchen cloths
2 White pitchers
1 Small ice pitcher
1 Thermometer
1 Meat pounder

18 Individual vegetable dishes
3 Vegetable dishes, plane
4 Meat pie plates
2 Agate hand bowls
1 Pan cake turner

PUMP HOUSE

1 Small vice
1 Wood box
1 Shovel

2 Pipe cutters
1 Oil can

162

LAUNDRY

1 Clothes boiler
1 Pair flatting irons

2 Benches
Clothes pins

GUESTS BATH ROOM

1 Carpet Rug

AROUND ABOUT THE CAMP

12 Wire mats
3 Cocoanut mats
1 Rubber mat
1 Double coal box
1 Large coal box

3 Smuge pails
12 Tree lamps
1 Hanging lamp on Dock
1 Hand sleigh in shop
2 Step ladders

OIL ROOM

9 Double lamp burners
6 Single lamp burners
5 Lantern lamp burners
1 Tin dipper
1 Box wicks mixed
3 Brass lanterns
2 Post lamps

2 Large oil tanks
1 Two quart measure
1 Funnel
1 Glass oil can feeder
8 Lanterns
2 Tree lamps
1 Port Lamp
1 Starboard lamp

NEW TABLE LINEN

3 Tray cloths

21 Doylies

10 Napkins

BLACKSMITH SHOP

1 Grinding stone
1 Portable forge
1 Anvil

1 Vice
1 Hammer
1 Chair

WORK SHOP

2 Gouges
4 Chisels
4 Cold chisels
2 Files
1 Wood saw
1 Rip saw
2 Hand saws
1 Keyhole saw
1 Mintor saw
3 Bits and bit stock
1 Hand axe
1 Oil stone
1 Mallet
1 Sledge hammer
1 Lath hatchet

3 Cross cut saws
4 Planes
2 Iron hedges [?]
1 Compass
2 Small squares
1 Two foot square
1 Wrench
1 Screw driver
1 Small Anvil
1 Draw shave
2 Augers
2 Hammers
1 Masons hammer
1 Masons trowel

BARN

1 Corn hiller and corn plough combine
3 Shovels
7 Bog hoes
5 Pick axes
2 Spading Forks
1 Grass edger
1 Lawn mower
1 Roof broom
1 Roof scraper

4 Ladders
1 Grub hoe
18 Flower pots
2 Axes
1 Garden trowl
1 Pair shears
12 Flower tubs
2 Lengths wire bound hose and hose cart

1 Light garden roller
2 Crowbars
3 Snow shovels
1 Post hole digger
1 Brush hook
3 Shuffle hoes
2 Wheel barrows
1 Length rubber hose

BARN BED ROOM

1 Carriage Lantern
1 Lamp

1 Clock
1 Mirror

BACHELORS' COTTAGE

1 Large rug
2 Single beds
2 Single springs
2 Single cotton mattresses
2 Single hair mattresses
4 Pillows
3 Tables
1 Japanese screen
2 Wash stands
2 Toilet sets
1 Bath tub and rubber bath sheet
1 Rocking chair
1 Arm chair
1 Straight chair
1 Wardrobe
1 Hanging cupboard
1 Wood box
2 Pairs snow shoes

1 Pair andirons
1 Set fire irons and stand
1 Fire screen
1 Lamp
2 Candlesticks
1 Deers head
2 Pairs red curtains
1 Door red curtains
2 Mirrors
1 Pair candle brackets
1 Brass lantern
2 Sponge racks
2 Shaving mugs
2 Pictures
1 Writing pad
1 Writing paper holder
1 Tray with ice water pitcher and glass
1 Table cloth

MRS. W. W. DURANT'S HOUSE

_____

SITTING ROOM

1 Brown carpet
1 Rug
1 Writing desk (rustic)
1 Sofa
3 Sofa pillows
2 Rustic tables
1 Rustic gun rack
1 Rocking chair
2 Arm chairs

1 Wall bookcase
1 Window seat cushion
2 Pairs red curtains
1 Door curtain
1 Pair red portieres
1 Japanese screen
1 Pair andirons
1 Wire fire screen
1 Set fire irons

164

1 Wicker chair
1 Solid wood chair

4 Stuffed birds
1 Wood box

BED ROOM

1 Green carpet
2 Single rustic beds
2 Single springs
2 Single hair mattresses
2 Single cotton mattresses
3 Small rugs
1 Arm chair
1 Rocking chair
3 Bureaus
1 Mirror

1 Brass lamp
2 Candle brackets
1 Wood box
2 Pairs red curtains
1 Fire screen
1 Pair andirons
1 Set fire irons
1 Brass kettle
1 Clothes hamper
1 Electric bell

BATH ROOM

1 Comode
1 Bebe [?]
2 Paper bowls
2 Soap dishes
2 Tooth glasses
1 Stationary bath

1 Towel rack
1 Bathtub seat
2 Foot tubs
1 Hanging cupboard
1 Sponge rack

STOVE ROOM

1 Stove with coil of pipe for heating water
1 Blacking stand
1 Fire pail
1 Hot water can
1 Brass candlestick
1 Galvanized Iron boiler

MRS. T. C. DURANT'S HOUSE

1 Red carpet
1 Large rug
2 Pair red curtains
1 Double rustic bed and springs
1 Double hair mattress
2 Double cotton mattresses
1 Bolster
2 Pillows
1 Sofa
1 Sofa pillow
2 Rustic tables
1 Wicker table
1 Rustic book-case
1 Electric bell

1 Cupboard
5 Chairs
1 Fire screen (wire)
1 Pair andirons
1 Wood box
1 Pair tongs
1 Poker
1 Bellows
1 Lamp (brass)
1 Lantern (brass)
1 Candle stick
1 Rustic clock
1 Tray, 1 Ice water pitcher and
  one tumbler

DRESSING ROOM

1 Rug
1 Dressing-table
1 Mirror
1 Pair red curtains
1 Chair
1 Wood box
1 Paper basket
2 Chambers
2 Tooth glasses
2 Soap dishes
2 Candle brackets

STOVE-ROOM

1 Stove, fitted with coil of pipes
1 Fire bucket
1 Galvanized iron boiler

BATH-ROOM

1 Stationary bath tub
1 Chair
2 Foot tubs
1 Hot water case
3 Red curtains

LONG NURSERY HALL

Linen cupboards
1 Fire bucket
Folding steps
1 Broom
1 Dustpan
1 Lantern

NURSERY HALL

1 Brown tin washstand
1 Brass lantern
1 Yellow silk door curtain
1 Carpet

BIG NURSERY

1 Large rug
1 Small rug
2 Single beds and springs
2 Hair mattresses
2 Cotton mattresses
2 Pillows
1 Folding bed (complete)
1 Large Bureau

1 Wash stand
1 Toilet set
1 Table
1 Coal stove
1 Brass screen
5 Chairs
1 Mirror
1 Wire fire screen

1 Pair andirons
1 Wood box
1 Pair tongs
1 Shovel
1 Bellows
2 Paper screens
1 Lamp
3 Pairs yellow silk curtains
1 Yellow door curtain

SMALL NURSERY

1 Carpet
1 Bed and springs
1 Hair mattress
1 Cotton mattress
1 Pillow
1 Bureau
1 Wash stand

1 Cupboard
2 Tables
3 Chairs
2 Pairs yellow silk curtains
1 Yellow silk door curtain
1 Wire fire screen
1 Pair andirons

1 Wood box
1 Tongs
1 Bellows
1 Toilet set
1 Paper bowl
1 Mirror
1 Lamp

GOVERNESS'S ROOM

1 Carpet
1 Single bed and spring
1 Hair mattress
1 Cotton mattress
1 Pillow   1 Stove

1 Washstand, complete
1 Wood-box   1 Book-case   2 chairs
1 Mirror
2 Pictures
1 Lamp

Index

Adirondack Company, 5, 9, 10, 85, 89, 91, 94, 95, 135. *See also* Adirondack Railway Company
Adirondack Ecological Center, 138
Adirondack Estate and Railroad Company, 9
Adirondack Forest Preserve, 11,
Adirondack Hardware Company, 107
Adirondack Museum, 11, 24, 51, 52, 53, 58, 105, 142
Adirondack Park, 10
Adirondack Railroad, 87, 132, 135
Adirondack Railway Company, 7, 9, 21, 88, 89, 94, 95, 133, 134. *See also* Adirondack Company
Adirondack Timber and Mineral Company, 135
"The Adirondacs" (poem), 110
Albany, 8, 11, 12, 14, 20, 52, 60, 85, 86, 93, 104, 108, 137, 140
Albany Medical College, 8
Alden, Seth, 137
Ames, Oakes, 2
Ames, Oliver, 2, 3
Anderson, John Jr., 137
Applegate, Howard, 107
Arbutus Lake, 137, 138
Arbutus Lake Camp (Mossy Camp), 96, 104, 137, 138
Arbutus Lake Preserve, 137, 138
Armour, Allison V., 104
Atterbury, Grosvenor, 100, 109

Baker, Gloria, 106, 107
Baker, R. T., 107
Ballard, John, 59
Banker, John T., 134
Barbour, John L., 87, 90, 132, 133, 134
Barque of Pine Knot (scow houseboat), 21, 22, 104
Beach, Judge Miles, 132, 135, 136
Benedict (family), 104
Benedict, Farrand, 4, 5
Benedict, George W., 4
Bennett, Edward, 53, 54
Bennett, Charles, 20, 53, 54
Bennett, Richard, 53
Berkeley Lodge, 55
Berton, Monsieur, 90

Bierstadt, Albert, 51
Bierstadt, Edward, 7, 20, 51, 53, 57
Big Island, 54
Birch Bark from the Adirondacks, Or From City to Trail, 7
Black, Governor Frank S., 97, 108
Blue Mountain Lake, 5, 11, 23, 50, 59, 86, 87, 89, 98, 140, 143, 145
Blue Mountain Land Company, 142
Bluff Point (Raquette Lake), 13, 58
Bonchee, Mrs., 60
Bradley, Henry ("Commodore"), 94
Brandreth Park, 52
Brezee, R. Newton, 100, 137
Brightside (Stott home, Stottsville), 60
Brightside-On-Raquette, 24
Broadway Magazine, 6
Brooklyn Eagle, 110
Brooklyn, N.Y., 85, 88, 110, 133
Brown, Augustus C., 135
Brown, Henry, 55
Bryere, Clara, 24
Bryere, Joseph O. A., 24, 55, 59, 60
Burnham, Hank, 99
Burns, M. Edward, 99, 140, 141
Buttercup (steamboat), 5

Callahan, John, 98, 100
Callahan, Mary, 98, 143
Callahan, Maurice, 95, 137, 141, 146
Callahan, Thomas, 98, 107
Camp Cedars, 50, 51, 52, 53, 54, 57
Camp Echo. *See* Echo Camp
Camp Endion (Long Lake), 52
Camp Fairview, 14, 24, 50, 52–55, 57
Camp Omonsom, 25, 108, 109. *See also* Kamp Kill Kare
Camp Pine Knot, 3, 11, 13, 19–25, 50, 51, 53, 54, 57, 58, 59, 60, 85, 93, 94, 95, 97, 99, 100, 101, 102, 106, 108, 109, 132, 137, 138, 141, 142, 146
Camp Sagamore. *See* Sagamore Lodge
Camp Stott, 24, 53, 57–60, 101
Camp Uncas, 22, 24, 95, 97, 98, 100–106, 108, 109, 135, 138, 142, 144
Camps, Adirondack. *See* Arbutus Lake Camp, Berkeley Lodge, Camp Cedars, Camp Endion, Camp Fairview, Camp Omonsom, Camp Pine

Knot, Camp Stott, Camp Uncas, Echo Camp, Kamp Kill Kare, Little Forked Camp, Sagamore Lodge
Carnegie, Mrs. Lucy, 107
Caughnawaga Club, 137
Cedars, *See* Camp Cedars
Central Pacific Railroad, 2, 96
Central Park, 3, 6, 19, 110
Chicago and Rock Island Railroad, 9
Choate, Joseph H., 93, 95
Civil War, 11, 22, 51, 110
Civilian Conservation Corps, 145
Clearwater, N.Y., 60, 100, 104, 140
Cleveland, Grover, 55
Collier, Robert J., 13, 58, 60, 103, 110
Collins, Margaret, 98
Collins, Richard J., 97, 98
Colvin survey, 14
Colvin, Verplanck, 14, 93
Constable family, 4
Constitution of 1894 (N.Y.), 141
Cooper, James Fenimore, 100
Corsair (yachts), 91, 100
Cotterill, C. W., 93
Cottier & Company, 99
Cotton, Annie. *See* Durant, Annie Cotton
Coulter, William L., 100, 107, 109
Count La Salle, 91
Craftsman Movement, 53
Crane, Edward, 89, 135
Crane, Henry C., 89
Crèdit Mobilier, 2, 3, 90
Cromley, Robert W., 134, 135
Cronk, Charles E., 55
"Cyclopean" Style, 112

Dante, A Dramatic Poem, 145
Dante, Alighieri, 85
Dante Society of America, 145
Davis, Dave, 99
Davison, Charles Stewart, 136
De Forest, Richard W., 95
De Forest, Robert, 93, 100
Delaware & Hudson Bulletin, 87
Delaware and Hudson Canal Company, 89, 91, 132, 134, 135
Distin, William G., 107
Dix, Governor John A., 86

Dix, Mrs. John A., 86
Dix, William Frederick, 99
Donaldson, Alfred L., 20, 21
Dougherty, Charles, 98, 137
Douglas, Senator, 140
Ducal Skeleton, A, 145
Dunning, Alvah, 12, 13, 19, 20, 51, 52, 53, 105
Durant, Annie Cotton, 105, 144, 145
Durant, Charles Wright, 8, 58, 87
Durant, Charles W. Jr., 12, 13, 14, 52, 53, 55, 58
Durant (family), 1, 2, 3, 5, 8, 10, 11, 14, 19, 21, 50, 52, 53, 54, 57, 58, 59, 85, 86, 94, 97, 132, 133, 134, 135, 144, 145
Durant, Frederick Clark, 50, 52, 58
Durant, Mrs. Frederick Clark, 50, 52
Durant, Frederick Clark Jr., 51
Durant Geneology, 145
Durant, Heloise Hannah (Ella), 1–3, 85, 86, 87, 88, 89, 90, 91, 92, 93, 94, 95, 104, 132–136, 137, 142, 144, 145, 146
Durant, Heloise Hannah Timbrell (Mrs. Thomas Clark Durant), 2, 9, 13, 21, 85, 86, 87, 90, 91, 94, 132, 133, 134, 136, 145
Durant, Howard Marion, 57, 58, 87
Durant, Janet Stott Lathrop, 13, 60, 86, 88, 90, 91, 95, 103, 144
Durant, Kenneth, 52, 53
Durant, Lathrop & Company, 8, 86
Durant, Dr. Thomas Clark, 1–14, 20, 50, 51, 58, 60, 85–88, 90, 91, 93, 94, 95, 96, 132, 133, 134, 135, 136, 143, 145, 146
Durant, Mrs. Thomas Clark. *See* Durant, Heloise Hannah Timbrell
Durant, William Franklin, 8
Durant, William West, 1, 3–6, 10–14, 55, 57, 58, 60; Camps, construction of; Arbutus Lake (Mossy Camp), 137–139; Cedars, 50, 51; Fariview, 52, 53; Kill Kare, 108, 110, 112; Sagamore, 104–107; Uncas, 100–102; Uncas, Sagamore, Kill Kare, 97–99; family matters, 85–88; Forest Park Land Company, 94, 95; later years, 144–146; Raquette Lake Railroad, 140–143; relationship with Collis P. Huntington, 95, 96; with Ella Durant, 89–92; Sale of Adirondack Railway Company, 89; suit of 1895, 93, 94; trial of 1899, 132–136
Durkee, C. E., 87
Duryea Camp, 98

Eagle Bay, N.Y., 100
Eagle Nest (Eagle's Nest), 105, 142, 144
Eagle's Nest Country Club, 140

Echo Camp, 50, 52, 54, 55, 108
Eckford Chain of Lakes, 1, 5, 142
Edwards, A. F., 4
"Eherhardt and Cotterill," 13
Ehrehart, J. H., 14
Emerson, Frank, 59
Emerson, Mrs. Margaret, 103, 107
Emerson, Ralph Waldo, 110
Endion. *See* Camp Endion
Episcopal Church (St. Hubert's Island), 59
Equitable Loan and Trust Company, 3

Fairview. *See* Camp Fairview
Farten, Frank, 24, 25
Fartin, A., 108
Field and Stream, 109
Fish Camp, 108
Fisher, Andrew, 52, 53
Flynn, Frank, 99
Follensby Pond, 10
Forest Commission, 12, 14
Forest Park and Land Company, 94, 95, 96, 134, 141, 142
Forest Preserve, 14, 103, 104, 141
Forest Preserve Board, 104, 105
"Forever Wild" (Article 14), 14, 141
Forked Lake, 50, 51, 55
Forked Lake House (hotel), 1
Fowler, George, 12
Frethey, Arthur B., 90
Frethey, Heloise H., 93. *See also* Durant, Heloise Hannah (Ella)
Fulton Chain of Lakes, 5, 98

"The Gables" (North Creek), 3, 60, 85, 86
Garvan, Dr. Anthony N. B., 110, 112
Garvan (family), 98, 99, 108, 110, 111
Garvan, Francis P., 110, 112
Garvan, Mrs. Francis P., 111, 112
Gates, Isaac Edwin ("Brother Gates"), 96, 140, 141, 143
Gerster, Dr. Arpad, 25, 54, 94, 100, 104, 105, 108, 109
Gerster (family), 109
Gerster, John, 108
Glaser-Kirschenbaum, Howard and Barbara, 103
Gleason, George M., 8
Goodenow, Mountain and Preserve, 137, 139
Great Blowdown (Nov., 1950), 52
Green-Wood Cemetery, 88, 90, 145

Hall, Amos, 132
Hamilton County, 9, 12, 94, 95, 136, 145
Hammond, W. J., 137, 138
Harpers Weekly, 51
Harrison, President Benjamin, 55

Harrison, Joseph Jr., 50
Hatch, Judge, 136
Havinga, Mrs. Francis, 55
Helms, David, 1
Helms, William, 1
Henderson, John B., 55
Henderson, Mary F., 143
Herkimer, N.Y., 55, 140, 141
Hewitt, Abram S., 93, 135
Hiscoe, Charles (Captain), 109, 110
History of the Adirondacks, A, 20
Hochschild, Harold K., 4, 10, 20, 50, 51, 53, 54, 55, 58, 91, 92, 103, 141, 142, 144
Hochschild, Walter, 144
Hoffman, Governor, 8
Holkham Hall, 50
Honnedaga Lake, 56
Hoppin, C. M., 6
Hoy, Mr. and Mrs. Johnny, 99
Huntington, Anna Vaughn, 138, 139
Huntington, Archer, 137, 138, 139
Huntington, Archer and Anna, Wildlife Forest Station, 138
Huntington, Collis P., 20, 21, 22, 23, 53, 60, 89, 94, 95, 96, 99, 100, 104, 137, 139, 140, 141, 142, 143
Huntington, Mrs. Collis P., 95, 137
Huntington, Helen Gates, 138

Independent, The, 99
Indian Lake, 53, 143
Inman, Horace, 13

Jamaica Estates, 144
Jenkins, George, 60
Jones, Freeland, 98

Kamp Kill Kare, 22, 24, 54, 97, 98, 99, 100, 102, 104, 105, 108–112. *See also* Camp Omonsom
Kathan, Schuyler, 23, 99
Kenwall, Ike, 59
Kwenogamac (camp), 109

Ladew (family), 144
Ladew, Joseph Harvey, 13, 53
Lake Durant, 145
Lake Harris House (Newcomb), 144
Lake Kora, 97, 104, 108, 110, *See also* Sumner Lake
Lake Lila, 101
Lake Ontario and Hudson River Railroad Company, 9
Land Board, 13
Land Office, 9, 12, 13, 14
Last of the Mohicans, The, 100
Lathrop, 86
Leavitt, George, 1
Leffler, James, 98
Lewis & Conger, 23

Lincoln, President Abraham, 6
Little Forked Camp, 56, 57, 58
Little Forked Lake, 52, 57
Little, Frank, 98, 99
Little, Jerry, 108
Little Osprey Island, 53
Lloyd, Joseph P., 96
Locke, Willard, 59
London, England, 3, 10, 90, 91, 92, 134
Long Lake, N.Y., 4, 5, 6, 21, 54, 60, 104, 108, 109, 137, 143, 144
Long Lake, 4
Long Point (Raquette Lake), 3, 20, 54
Long View House (Long Lake), 144
Lounsbury, Governor Phineas C., 50, 54, 55, 108
Lusitania (ship), 107

Macomb, Alexander, 10, 11
Mahan, Dennis, 59
March, Dr. Alden, 8
Marion River Carry, 1, 3, 55
Marion River Carry Railroad, 142
Marshall, Senator Henry, 105
Marshall, William, 101
Maxam, Fred ("Mossy"), 99
Merchants Exchange National Bank, 54
Millington, Douglas, 99
Mix, Alonzo, 20
Mohegan Lake, 97, 100, 101, 102
Molineaux, Miss, 85, 90, 94
Morgan, Anne, 102, 103
Morgan, J. Pierpont, 91, 95, 98, 102, 103, 105, 107, 140, 141, 143
Morgan, J. P. ("Jack"), 103
Mossy Camp. *See* Arbutus Lake Camp
Murphy, Frances, 86, 88, 133
Murray, William ("Adirondack"), 12

National Arts Club, 145
National Humanistic Education Center, 103, 107
Neafie & Levy, 91
Ne-Ha-Sa-Ne (camp and park), 99, 101
Nevins, Allan, 3
New York City, 1, 2, 3, 6, 7, 8, 9, 19, 21, 24, 50, 54, 56, 85, 86, 88, 89, 91, 94, 99, 100, 108, 110, 132, 136, 138, 144, 145
New York, Constitution, 141
New York Daily Times, 4, 6
New York Daily Tribune, 5, 94, 110, 145
New York State, 4, 5, 9–14, 96, 103, 104, 107, 109, 144
New York Times, The, 91, 95, 103, 136, 144
New York Yacht Club, 58, 91
Newcomb, 137, 138, 139, 144
Nicholas, Admiral Edward T., 58

North Creek, 3, 5, 6, 9, 60, 85, 86, 87, 89, 133, 134, 137, 138
North River, 9, 137
Norwood, Carlisle, 132

Odell, Daniel, 89, 94, 133
Old Forge, N.Y., 5, 55, 98
Osprey (boat), 53
Osprey Island, 12, 13, 14, 19, 20, 52, 53, 144
Ostrander, George, 144
Outdoor Education Center, State University of New York, Cortland, 20, 22
Owens, Frank, 99

Palmer, Lucius N., 132
Panic of 1876, 3
Parker, Alvin, 53, 55
Parker, Darwin, 53
Parsons, John E., 132, 134
Parsons, Shepard & Ogden, 93, 132
Pashley, George, 53
Pierce, Seth, 51, 53
Pine Knot. *See* Camp Pine Knot
Pine Needles or Sonnets and Songs, 85, 145
Pirong, Francis, 99
Poland Committee, 3
Pope, Alexander, 19
Pope, John Russell, 111, 112
Porter, Sidney, 59
Powers, Hiram, 2
Pratt, Dr. Richmond, 95
Preservation League of New York, 107
Price-Waterhouse, 142
Promontory Point, Utah, 2, 4
Prospect House, 50, 58, 59
Prospect Park (Brooklyn), 19, 110, 133

Queen Anne Style, 53, 58, 101

Raines, Senator, 140
Raquette Falls Land Company, 142
Raquette Lake, 1, 3–6, 11, 13, 14, 19, 20, 23, 24, 52–55, 58, 59, 87, 97, 98, 100, 103–105, 108, 112, 137, 141, 143–145
Raquette Lake Railroad (Railway), 13, 140, 142, 143, 144
Raquette Lake Transportation Company, 55, 142
Raquette River, 4, 5, 6
Raymond, Henry Jarvis, 4, 5
Rexford, James B., 137
Rich Lake (Newcomb), 137, 139, 143
Robertson, Robert, 101
Roblee, Albert, 98
Rockland County (N.Y.) Council of the Boy Scouts of America, 103

Rogers, Garry, 98, 137
Root. Elihu, 95
Rose, Charles Henry Marcus, 89, 94
Rose, Mrs. Charles Henry Marcus. *See* Durant, Heloise Hannah (Ella)
Rose, Timbrell Durant, 94, 145
Ryan, W. C. M., 99

Sackets Harbor & Saratoga Railroad Company, 4, 5, 9
Sagamore Lake, 98, 104, 105, 106. *See also* Shedd Lake
Sagamore Lodge (Camp Sagamore), 24, 97–107, 109, 137, 138, 142
Sagamore Preserve, 99, 100, 103, 109, 142
St. Hubert's Island, 52, 59, 60
Saranac Lake, N.Y., 100, 107
Saratoga Springs, 3, 6, 9, 11, 85, 86, 87, 100, 137
Seymour, General Silas, 87
Shedd Lake, 55, 97, 104. *See also* Sagamore Lake
Shingle Style, 101
Simpson, Harry W., 132
Smith and Simpson, 132
Smith, Freling H., 132, 134
Smith, Joe, 99
Smith, Josh, 98, 99, 108, 137
Sneed Creek, 108
Snyder, Charles E., 141, 144, 145
Southern Pacific Railway, 21, 95
Starbuck, George, 99
Steadman, Edmund C., 6
Stella (boat), 53
Stoddard, Seneca Ray, 19, 20, 24, 60, 100, 105, 106, 137
Stott. *See* Camp Stott
Stott (family), 60, 86, 97, 103
Stott, Frank H., 13, 58, 59
Stott, Mrs. Frank H., 59, 60
Stott, Janet Lathrop. *See* Durant, Janet Lathrop Stott
Stottville, N.Y., 58, 60
Sumner Lake, 97, 108, 109. *See also* Lake Kora
Sunset Land, The, 4
Suplee, H. H., 57
Sutphen, William, 88, 134
Syracuse University, 103, 107

Taylor, Frank H., 7
Thompson, J. George, 55, 143
Tillson, John E., 21
Todd, Reverend John, 4, 5
Town & Country Magazine, 99
Township 5, 97, 135, 141
Township 6, 95, 97, 104, 108, 135, 141
Township 34, 135

Township 34 (book), 4, 20, 50, 54, 58, 91, 103, 142, 144
Township 40, 4, 11, 12, 13, 14, 141
Township 41, 141
Truax, Chauncey, 89
Tuttle, Ollie, 103
Tweed, Charles H., 141
Twickenham School, England, 2, 19

Uncas. *See* Camp Uncas
Uncas Estates, Inc., 103
"Under the Hemlocks" (hotel), 54
Union Pacific Railroad, 1, 2, 8, 9, 85, 87, 91
U.S. Department of Agriculture, 141
Utowana (yacht), 91, 92, 93, 95, 100, 104, 143, 146

Van Valkenburgh, Norman, 11
Vanderbilt, Alfred G., 99, 103, 107, 110, 142
Vanderbilt (family), 99
Vanderbilt, George, 107
Vanderbilt, Margaret McKim Emerson. *See* Emerson, Mrs. Margaret
Venice (gondola), 110

Wack, Henry Wellington, 98, 109
Wallace, Fred, 98
Wallace, Thomas, 59, 60
Warrensburg-Lake George News, 24
Webb, John Beavor, 91, 100
Webb, Dr. William Seward, 6, 101, 140, 141, 142
Whipple, James S., 97, 105, 109

White, Stanford, 56
Whitney, C. V., 52
Whitney, H. C., 140
Whitney, Mrs. Harry Payne, 52
Whitney Park, 52
Whitney, William C., 140, 141
Wilson, George, 99
Woodruff, Cora, 108, 109, 110
Woodruff, Lieut. Governor Timothy L., 95, 100, 104, 105, 108, 109, 110, 140, 144
Wood, Jerome, 59
Wright, George, 99

Yale College, 107

Zack Lake and Preserve, 137

170

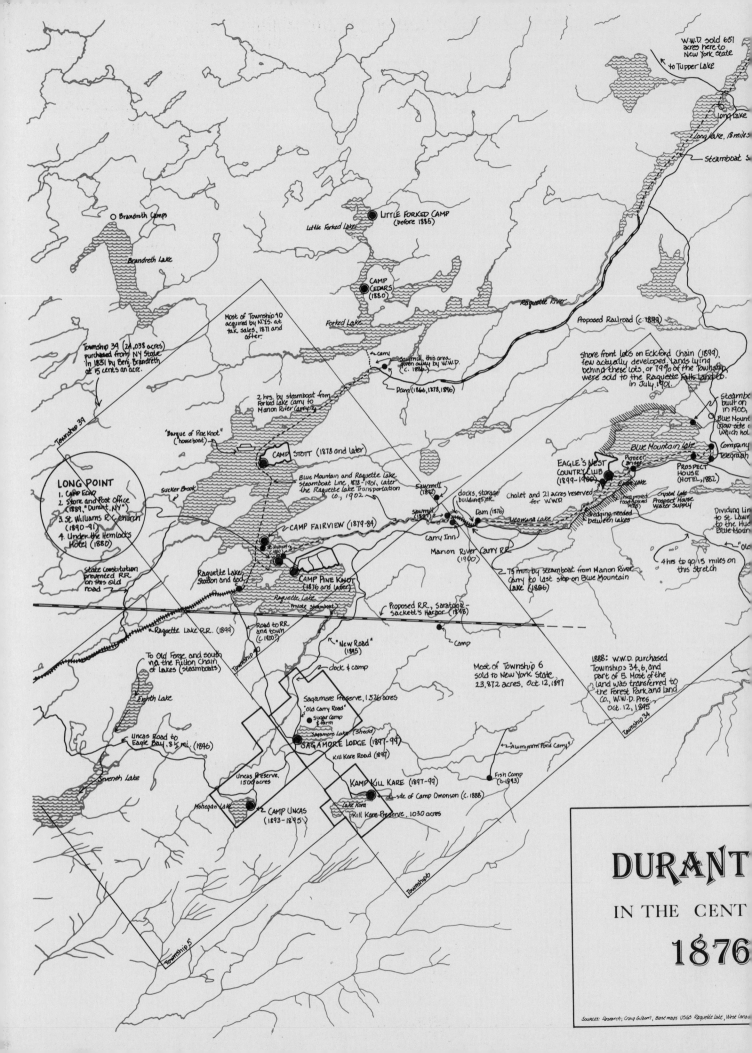